Emerging Leadership

SPIRITUAL FORMATION: THE FOUNDATION

Stanley E. Granberg

Spiritual Formation—Strengthening Leadership Foundations
copyright © 2012 Stanley E. Granberg

Requests for information should be addressed to:

KairosTraining@kairoschurchplanting.org

11124 NE Halsey #497
Portland, OR 97220

All scripture quotations, unless otherwise indicated, are taken from the *Holy Bible, New International Version*®, NIV®. Copyright ©1973, 1978, 1984, 2011 by Biblica, Inc.™ Used by permission of Zondervan. All rights reserved worldwide. www.zondervan.com.

The "NIV" and *"New International Version"* are trademarks registered in the United States Patent and Trademark Office by Biblica, Inc.™

Scripture taken from the HOLY BIBLE, TODAY'S NEW INTERNATIONAL VERSION®. Copyright © 2001, 2005 by Biblica®. Used by permission of Biblica®. All rights reserved worldwide.

"TNIV" and *"Today's New International Version"* are trademarks registered in the United States Patent and Trademark Office by Biblica®. Use of either trademark requires the permission of Biblica.

All rights reserved. No part of this publication may be reproduced, stored in a retrieval system, or transmitted in any form or by any means without the prior permission of Kairos Church Planting.

Cover design by Bethany Cannon

Contents

Letter of Welcome	iii
Self-Study Schedule and Exercise List	iv
The Emerging Leader Training Process	v

Spiritual Formation — 1

Lesson 1: About this Module — 1
- Module Objectives: Action Steps — 2
- Missional Director Meetings — 3

Unit A: Your Experience — 5

Lesson 2: Assessing Your Leadership Experience — 5
- Reading: Barton, chapters 1-2 — 5
- Initial Screening Assessment — 7

Lesson 3: Missional Leadership — 10
- Reading: Barton, chapters 3-4 — 10
- Missional Leader Inventory — 10

Unit B: Your Walk With God — 17

Lesson 4: Developing Spiritual Habits — 17
- Reading: Barton chapters 5-6 — 17
- "The Daily Office" — 18

Lesson 5: Leading With Prayer — 21
- Organize a Prayer Team — 21
- My Personal Prayer Team — 24

Lesson 6: Considering Your Life — 25
- Reading: Barton chapters 7-8 — 25
- Timelines — 25
- A Calling Timeline — 27
- Your Personal Calling Timeline — 31

Unit C: Your Heart Passions   33

Lesson 7: Your Heart Passions   33

   Reading: Barton chapters 9-10   34

   Your Passion Bulls-eye   34

   Changing Passions   37

Lesson 8: Protect Your Health   40

   Reading: Barton chapters 11-13   40

   Protect Your Physical Health   40

   Protect Your Integrity   45

   Ethical Conduct Agreement   46

Unit D: Your Personality   49

Lesson 9: Your Personality—The Golden/MBTI   49

   Reading: Peterson, Introduction   49

   The Golden/MBTI   50

   Digging Deeper into the Golden   51

   Personality Type Groups   53

Lesson 10: Your Personality—The Portrait Predictor/DiSC   55

   Reading: Peterson, chapters 1-3   55

   The Portrait Predictor/DiSC   55

   Missional Director Meeting   57

Unit E: Your Giftedness   59

Lesson 11: Thinking Through Giftedness   59

   Reading: Peterson, chapters 4-6   59

   Types of Giftedness   60

Lesson 12: Spiritual Gifts   64

   Illustrate Your Giftedness Set   67

Unit F: Practicing Spiritual Disciplines   71

Lesson 13: Disciplines and World Engagement   71

   Reading: Peterson, chapters 7-9   72

   A Look at Spiritual Disciplines   72

Unit G: Strategy Assignment — 76
The Strategy Assignment Overview — 76

- Personal Development Plan — 76
- Worksheet 1 - Clarify Purpose: Surfacing Your Worldview Perspective — 80
- Worksheet 2 - Evaluate Experience: Your Leadership Timeline — 82
- Worksheet 3 - Identify Uniqueness: Understand Your Giftedness — 88
- Worksheet 4 - Define Identities: My Roles and Responsibilities — 91
- Worksheet 5 - Maximize Resources: Envision the Long Term — 95
- Worksheet 6 - Integrate Essentials: Write a Personal Life Mandate — 99
- Sample Personal Life Mandate, person age 30-40 — 99
- Worksheet 7 - Acquire Wisdom: Plan a Wisdom Future — 102

Letter of Welcome

Dear Emerging Leader,

You have been on my heart and mind for a long time now, though I may not know you personally. I may not know your plans, your dreams, or your hopes, but please know that I have been and continue to pray for you.

You have been on my heart because you are at the cutting edge of God's kingdom. God is preparing you for amazing ministry and work. At this point he has provided you a foundation. He gave you your unique personality. He provided you a network of people and experiences that have molded and formed you.

Now you are opening the next phase of your development. By choosing to participate in the Kairos Emerging Leader Training (ELT) series, you are saying you are serious about your development as a godly leader. You are asking those around you—your missional director, your church leaders, and significant people in your church body—to guide, instruct, help, and encourage you. You are placing yourself in God's hands to mold you through the set of experiences provided in the ELT series so you can become the leader he intends for you to be.

The vision of the Kairos ministry is to see a generation of 21st century churches arise. These new churches will need a variety of godly leaders: lead church planters, worship leaders, prayer leaders, missional community leaders, and committed Christians who know how to live a missional, kingdom lifestyle that shares Jesus in word and deed with the world around them. I believe you are one of these new leaders. The Kairos Emerging Leader Training series was written to provide you a starting point as you develop into a dynamic 21st century leader.

God bless you fully in your developing journey. Listen closely for his word to you. Open your heart to his heart. Let God's passions become yours.

I look forward to meeting you one day, if not here, then in God's eternal future as together we stand surrounded by the multitude of his people and sing, "I once was lost, but now I'm found."

In the love and power of the risen Lord,

Stan Granberg, PhD
Kairos Executive Director

Self-Study Schedule and Exercise List

This module will guide you through a process of self discovery. Use this schedule to plan your study. Begin each unit by reading the assigned book chapters. The core exercises are what you will do to develop the life skills that characterize a godly leader. As you complete the core exercises, you will compile your thoughts and experiences in the answer book. This answer book is available to download at kairoschurchplanting.org. At the end of this module, you will return the answer book to Kairos. This module is designed to take six months to complete. Look over your personal calendar and this workbook. Enter your expected completion date for each core exercise in the last column.

Unit	Lesson	Readings	Core Exercises	Date to Complete
	1 - About This Module		Missional Director Meeting #1	
A - Your Experience	2 - Assessing Your Leadership Experience 3 - Missional Leadership	Barton Chapters 1-4	ISA Missional Leader Inventory	
B - Your Walk With God	4 - Developing Spiritual Habits 5 - Leading With Prayer 6 - Considering Your Life	Barton Chapters 5-8	Practice the Daily Office Your Calling Timeline Organize a Prayer Team	
C - Your Heart Passions	7 - Your Heart Passions 8 - Protect Your Health	Barton Chapters 9-13	Passion Bulls-eye (actual) Passion Bulls-Eye (ideal) Ethical Conduct Agreement	
D - Your Personality	9 - The Golden/MBTI 10 - The Portrait Predictor/DiSC	Peterson Introduction	Golden/MBTI Portrait Predictor/DiSC Missional Director Meeting #2	
E - Your Giftedness	11 - Thinking Through Giftedness 12 - Spiritual Gifts	Peterson Chapters 1-3	Spiritual Gifts Inventory Giftedness Set	
F - Practicing Spiritual Disciplines	13 - Disciplines and World Engagement	Peterson Chapters 4-6	Spiritual Disciplines Inventory	
G - Strategy Assignment	14 - Personal Development Plan	Peterson Chapters 7-9	Personal Development Plan Missional Director Meeting #3	

The Emerging Leader Training Process

Background

The Emerging Leader Training (ELT) series is a product of Kairos Church Planting. The ELT is designed as a guided development process to engage emerging Christian leaders in leadership tasks that will grow their missional leadership skills. We have several purposes in providing the ELT:

- To provide emerging leaders with a guided process of personal development as a godly leader.
- To give planting churches a tool to raise up leaders and new church planters from among their members.
- To give new churches a tool for training future staff ministers, team leaders, apprentices, and church planters.
- To provide to those who have gone through a planter assessment a process for developing the skills they may still need to be ready to lead or be on a new church plant team.

ELT Content

The ELT series contains four modules spaced across two years. Year one modules cover basic leadership: 1) Spiritual Formation and 2) Sharing Faith. Year two covers leadership skills more intentionally focused on church planting through 3) Essential Leadership and 4) Leading by Design.

The modules are keyed to leadership skills assessed in the Emerging Leadership Initiative's Initial Screening Assessment (ISA), a skills inventory created to identify potential church planters. These skills are important skills for anyone who wishes to be a leader in 21st century churches. Sixty-eight of the eighty-five components measured in the ISA are addressed in the four ELT workbooks. In this workbook on Spiritual Formation you will work on the following skills measured by the ISA, skills associated with trying new things, taking risks and increasing your visioning capacity:

- I like creating new things, that involve finding new ways of solving problems.
- I am a risk taker.
- I like to explore new territory.
- I have the reputation for being a really hard worker.
- I tend to be competitive.
- I seem to be really good at envisioning something in my mind before it is actually taking place or built.

When you complete the two-year ELT you will have raised your skill level as a missional Christian leader and your scores on the ISA.

Working with an ELT Module

Each module includes the following elements to facilitate adult learning:

- **Reading:** Core reading provides essential content for each module.

- **Workbook:** The heart of the module is this workbook. The workbook presents important insights and guided exercises that will develop your missional leadership skills. The workbook is yours to keep.

- **Personal Answer Book:** Download a copy of your personal answer book at http://kairoschurchplanting.org/resources/emerging-leader-training/ Print a copy. This booklet includes the core exercises you will complete as you go through the module workbook. At the end of this module, send your personal answer book to Kairos at 11124 NE Halsey St. #497, Portland, OR 97220 to receive your certificate of completion.

- **Webinar:** Periodically, experienced church plant leaders will lead webinars from their own missional experiences and experiments—what worked, what didn't and what they've learned along the way. You can access these webinars at kairoschurchplanting.org under resources.

- **Missional Director:** In your church context you will work under the guidance of a missional director, typically a church staff minister, who will monitor your progress, help you process your reading and experiences, and direct you as you practice missional leadership.

- **Strategy Assignment:** Each module culminates in a strategy assignment that applies your learning in an integrated activity. The strategy assignement is the most important exercise in the module.

Completing an ELT Module

To complete an ELT module you must successfully accomplish the following:

- Complete the workbook and reading assignments.
- Receive positive evaluations from your missional director.
- Accomplish your strategy assignment.
- Email or mail your completed personal answer book to us at KairosTraining@kairoschurchplanting.org or 11124 NE Halsey St. #497, Portland, OR 97220.

x

Spiritual Formation

Lesson 1: About this Module

As you work through the Spiritual Formation module, you will assess where God has brought you thus far in your life, strengthen your spiritual life, and open yourself to God's preferred future for you as he molds you into a Christian leader. The module is arranged in six Units with a culminating strategy assignment, all to be completed over a four month time period. This module consists of four essential components:

1. **Reading: Purchase the following books**
- Ruth Haley Barton, *Strengthening the Soul of Your Leadership*. IVP, 2008
- Eugene Peterson, *Working the Angles: The Shape of Pastoral Integrity*. Eerdmans, 1987.

2. **Workbook**

This workbook is your primary guide. It is designed with questions and exercises for you to complete. You will keep the workbook as a record of your spiritual journey into leadership.

3. **Answer Book**

Download a copy of your personal answer book at http://kairoschurchplanting.org/resources/emerging-leader-training/ and use it to re-complete the exercises in this workbook. On completing this module, send your personal answer book and strategy assignment materials to

Kairos Church Planting
11124 NE Halsey St. #497
Portland, OR 97220

4. **Strategy Assignment**

The strategy assignment integrates everything you've learned in the module into a summative activity. For this module you will write a Personal Development Plan for your spiritual growth. This is an opportunity for you to acknowledge what God has done in your life thus far and to join him in what he is preparing you for. This workbook is not meant to be completed all at once, but across four months. The purpose is to develop you as a godly leader, not merely to complete a course or set of requirements. Development takes time, energy, and reflection. You can't make yourself grow, but you can give yourself the opportunity to grow.

Module Objectives: Action Steps

The Spiritual Formation module is intended to help you take the next step in laying spiritual foundations for a lifetime of Christian leadership. You will work through the following areas of Christian foundations which will reveal your current level of experience and development as an emerging Christian leader.

Unit A—Your Experience
- ❏ Evaluate your experience as a Christian leader through the Church Planter Profile's ISA
- ❏ Identify areas of strength and weakness in your experience base

Unit B—Your Walk with God
- ❏ Begin practicing the Daily Office
- ❏ Develop a personal calling timeline
- ❏ Form a prayer team and develop a one year plan to engage them in your life

Unit C—Your Heart Passions
- ❏ Commit to protect your personal integrity before God and others through an Integrity Covenant
- ❏ Identify your Current Passion Wheel
- ❏ Plan your Ideal Passion Wheel

Unit D—Your Personality
- ❏ Use the Golden/MBTI to understand your personality type
- ❏ Use the Portrait Predictor/DiSC to comprehend how you work with the world and others

Unit E—Your Giftedness
- ❏ Complete a spiritual gifts inventory
- ❏ Illustrate your spiritual giftedness through a giftedness set

Unit F—Practicing Spiritual Disciplines
- ❏ Assess your spiritual disciplines
- ❏ Design a spiritual disciplines plan

Unit G—Strategy Assignment
- ❏ Write your Personal Development Plan

Missional Director Meetings

The Paul/Timothy model is a powerful example of the relationship between an experienced leader and an emerging leader. This model is more than just a mentoring relationship. It is a training relationship. Paul took Timothy with him as he engaged in his own ministry. As Timothy grew in experience, Paul assigned leadership tasks for Timothy to practice his own leadership abilities. Ultimately, Timothy, a mature leader in his own right, assumed the lead ministry role at Ephesus   (I Timothy).

We believe that having a training relationship in a church context will multiply your growth process. If you have yet to do so, identify a missional director in your church, preferably a staff minister. It could also be an elder or, in some cases, a leader in a specific ministry in your church. Your missional director should meet the following criteria:

- Be currently employed by your church, have a background as a church minister, or be recognized as a spiritual leader in your church.
- Be someone you respect and wish to learn from.
- Have the time and interest to do the following:
    - Monitor your progress.
    - Meet with you five times in the next six months for two hours each meeting.
    - Prepare for these meetings by reading the two assigned books and following along in the workbook as you work through the assignments.
    - Be available to talk over questions when you have them, recommend other resources to you, and open doors for other experiences he or she thinks will help you grow as a godly leader.

During your first meeting with your missional director, which you should have before the end of the first lesson, do the following:

- Pray together.
- Read the ELT Relationship Covenant in your personal answer book aloud together and sign it. If you are working towards a certificate of completion, photocopy the covenant page and send it to Kairos at 11124 NE Halsey St., #497, Portland, OR 97220. Or, scan and e-mail it to KairosTraining@kairoschurchplanting.org.
- Talk about your expectations and hopes for your development as a missional leader through the ELT and this module on Spiritual Formation. Discuss the following questions:

What are you excited about in this module on Spiritual Formation?

_____
_____
_____

What challenges do you anticipate?

_____
_____
_____

What goals do you have in mind for yourself?

_____
_____
_____

How do you anticipate this module impacting your leadership in your church?

_____
_____
_____

What outcomes do you anticipate?

_____
_____
_____

Look over your anticipated timeline for completing this module on page iv. Talk through the timing, potential interferences, and why you are committing to this learning experience.

Unit A
Your Experience

Lesson 2: Assessing Your Leadership Experience

I enjoy reading fantasy books where the story begins with a young person who is drawn into an adventure that challenges him beyond his abilities. The draw of the story is that as the character goes through the challenge, he finds himself growing, maturing into a person who is capable and experienced. I enjoy reading the biographies of great leaders for the same reason. A common thread in historical biographies is that these leaders do not begin famous. They start out young and inexperienced, but grow into the kind of people whom others recognize and follow.

Good leaders are the product of personality, experience, opportunities, and leadership skills. As you consider your formation as an emerging Christian leader, it's important that you recognize the qualities and skills you already have. In this module, you will take several personal inventories. One of these inventories is the Initial Screening Assessment, or ISA. The ISA was developed by the Emerging Leadership Initiative as a screening tool for potential church planters. Though developed for church planters, the ISA has broader application for entrepreneurial leadership in general. You will also complete the Missional Leader Inventory in this unit.

Reading: Barton, chapters 1-2

Ruth Haley Barton is one of the leading writers and practitioners of spiritual formation. She is founding president of the Transforming Center, a spiritual director, retreat leader, and author of several books on spiritual formation. For this module you will read her book, *Strengthening the Soul of Your Leadership*. Around the framework of Moses' life, Barton explores the core processes of spiritual formation in the life of a godly leader.

Read the foreword, introduction, and chapters 1-2. During this reading, I want you to do "impact journaling." All you need is some place to record your thoughts as you read. You could use a separate journal, a piece of paper tucked inside the book, your iPad, even the margins of Barton's book. The idea is to take note of what her ideas bring to your mind as you read.

Here are some examples:

- **Highlight or underline good quotes.** In the foreword, Leighton Ford does this. You can read his memorable quotes on page 10 of *Strengthening the Soul of Your Leadership*.

- **Jot down your emotional reactions.** Write an "amen," "right on," "nailed me," "no way," or other such statements. Use exclamation marks, question marks, stars, arrows, smiley faces, or whatever captures the emotion the reading evokes in you.

- **Record your questions.** What new questions does Barton raise in your mind? Write these down. Consider sharing them with your missional director over coffee.

- **Identify applications.** How will you use the ideas Barton writes about? Are specific events happening right now where you can practice something she talks about? Is there an ongoing practice you want to turn into a life habit?

- **Connect to scripture.** Because your attention is being directed by your reading, new ideas will surface in your understanding and application of God's word. When you make a connection between something you've read in Barton and some biblical passage, note the passage and the idea.

Let me call attention to one of Barton's statements for you to consider:

Spiritual leadership emerges from our willingness to stay involved with our own soul—that place where God's Spirit is at work stirring up our deepest questions and longings to draw us deeper into relationship with him. (p. 25)

With church planters we talk about the leadership journey this way: "The people you lead will only be able to go on their spiritual journey as far as you are willing to go on yours." This is not to say that the planter is the most spiritual or mature person in the church. No way! It does say that if the planter encounters an issue, a condition, an event in which he becomes stuck or resists engaging himself in God's purposes for his life, he should expect to see the church reflect that resistance as well. Your personal willingness to journey into the heart of God models the way others should and can make the journey too.

Over these next weeks and months, God may raise some resistance in your soul to your awareness. I pray for your courage to "stay involved with your own soul—that place where God's Spirit is at work…"

Initial Screening Assessment

The Emerging Leadership Initiative (ELI: elichurchplanting.com) is the brainchild of John Burke (author of *No Perfect People Allowed* and *Soul Revolution)* and Craig Whitney. Their aim with this tool is to inspire and mobilize new leaders to plant new churches. In 2008, ELI created Church Planter Profiles (CPP: churchplanterprofiles.com) to make a battery of leadership inventories available for church planting ministries. Kairos Church Planting is a registered agency with CPP. We use these inventories in our Discovery Lab assessment process.

ELI developed the Initial Screening Assessment (ISA) in 2006 to help identify potential church planters. The ISA assesses basic and advanced leadership experience. This is what we are interested in now. We want you to get a sense of your level of leadership experience. The ISA will ask you about your experiences in four categories: 1) church planting, 2) entrepreneurial leadership, 3) ministry experience, and 4) relational evangelism.

Action Step

- Go to churchplanterprofiles.com.
- Create your account.
- On the new account page, complete the form. At the bottom, select Kairos Church Planting as your church planting agency. This will notify us that you have created your account and will let us see your inventories as you complete them.
- To create your account you are required to take the Initial Screening Assessment.
- Once you have completed the ISA, download your ISA report. It will look something like the following, but with your name and scores of course.

Note: If you are a lay leader or a woman, do not be put off or dismayed as you take the ISA. It was designed for men who are in full-time ministry. Chances are you have not had the opportunities to do much of what the ISA measures. Still, you can expect to get valuable insights from this assessment.

The ISA uses traffic light colors to quickly identify experience levels.

Green indicates a significant amount of leadership experience. In the example below, the emerging leader is most developed in the area of church planting and has reached a threshold sufficient for green.

Yellow indicates a moderate level of experience. You may see that most of your scores fall into the yellow category.

Red indicates little experience. If you are a new Christian or young in age, some or all of your scores could be red.

Don't let a red score bother you. Remember, this is an experience-based inventory. It is showing that you have not yet accumulated sufficient experience in that area tfor a high score. As you work through the Emerging Leader Training (ELT) series, you will develop many leadership skills measured by the ISA. If you complete all four modules, you should expect to raise your scores significantly.

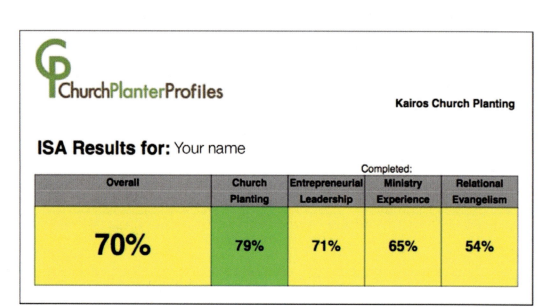

Reporting

Record your ISA scores on page 4 in your personal answer book.

When you look at your ISA results, what do you see that you expected?

_____
_____
_____
_____
_____
_____
_____
_____

What do you see that surprises you? Why?

_____
_____
_____
_____
_____
_____
_____
_____

What is the most significant insight into your leadership you gained from the ISA?

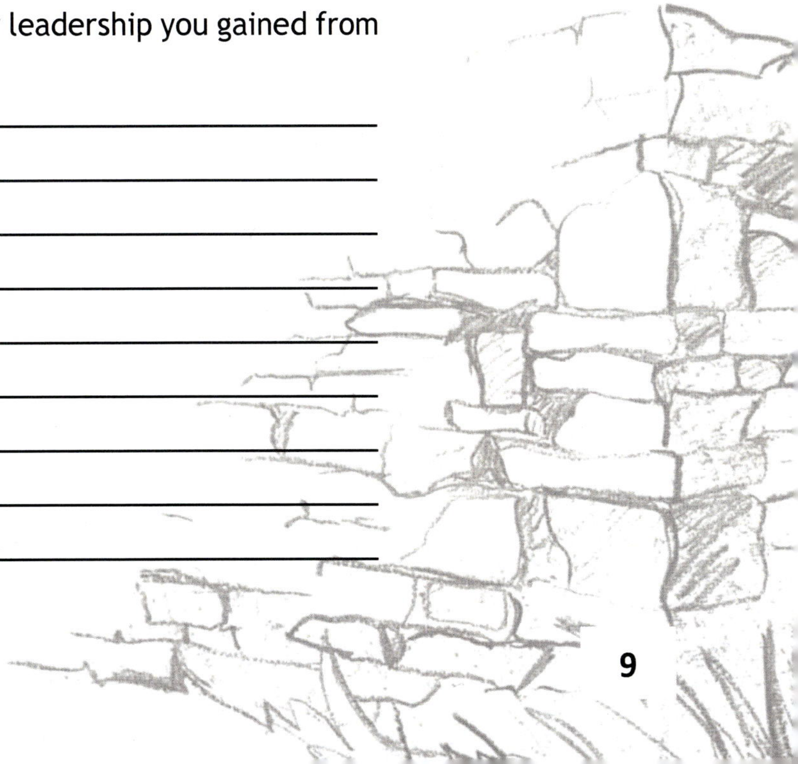

_____
_____
_____
_____
_____
_____
_____
_____

Lesson 3: Missional Leadership

Reading: Barton, chapters 3-4

In this week's readings Barton introduces three spiritual dynamics from Christian tradition: purgation, consolation, and desolation.

Purgation (Barton, p. 25) is the commitment to self-knowledge. It is part of the ongoing process of conversion in which the godly person empties him or herself in preparation to receive what God offers.

Consolation (Barton, p. 67) is the interior movement of the heart responding to God. It is the sense of God's life-giving presence, that we are right with God and the world.

Desolation (Barton, p. 67) is the loss of the sense of God's presence. Whether from sin, rebellion, or even apathy, when something interferes with our relationship with God, we lose the sense of his presence in our lives.

The godly leader can use these spiritual dynamics to take barometric readings on his or her spiritual life. Are you in a period of spiritually sunny weather, where all signs are positive? Or are storm clouds gathering or already dumping on you? You can learn to both prepare for and respond to life events by being aware of your spiritual barometer.

Missional Leader Inventory

Good research has been done on preparation and readiness for ministry. The Association of Theological Schools began a longitudinal research project in 1973 which continued until 2003. One of their findings is that there has been a "gradual, intensifying expectation that young ministers and priests both be more personally spiritual and witness their commitment to Christ in the congregations and parishes they serve."[1]

The Churches of God have also done significant thinking on the idea of readiness for ministry. They identified five areas of ministerial readiness: spiritual, intellectual, professional, emotional, and personal. Their study concludes, "A person is ready for ministry when readiness in these areas is integrated into readiness as a whole person for the pastoral calling."[2]

A third helpful resource is a personal assessment for ministry readiness compiled by Mary Alice Seals published as *Readiness for Ministry*.[3]

The Missional Leader Inventory combines insights from these three resources and from our organizational experience at Kairos. This inven-

---

1. Francis A. Lonsway, "Profiles of Ministry: A Thirty-Year Study," (Pittsburg: The Association of Theological Schools, 2007), 16.
2. Churches of God, General Conference, "Readiness for Ministry: Guidelines for Pastoral Maturity," Churches of God, General Conference, revised, (Findlay, OH: 2000), 4.
3. Mary Alice Seals, "Evaluation in the Supervisory Experience," in *Experiencing Ministry Supervision* (Nashville: B&H, 1995), 134-137.

tory will help you clarify your current readiness for church leadership. It will also give you a sense of the challenges of church leadership for the future. As you work through this inventory, think about your growth towards spiritual maturity as a godly leader.

Action Step

Read each item below and provide an answer using the following designations:

E = Excellent. I consider this area among my strengths/gifts.

S = Satisfactory. I have some experience in this area and do adequately perform the item.

US = UnSatisfactory. I have little experience in this area and cannot adequately perform the item.

UC = UnCertain. I am not sure at this time.

Missional Leader Inventory

Spiritual Life

_____ **Personal faith commitment in Jesus Christ?** I have made a decision of faith in Jesus Christ as Lord and Savior, evidenced by baptism and a changed life through Christ (Romans 6:1-4).

_____ **Personal spiritual discipline?** I maintain a regular schedule of private prayer, reading and reflecting on the Bible, and enriching my life with a variety of spiritual experiences and materials (1 Timothy 4:13-14).

_____ **Maintains a committed relationship with a community of faith?** I am an active part of a local congregation and I willingly submit myself to the authority of its spiritual leaders (Hebrews 10:23-25, 13:17; 2 Timothy 1:15-18).

_____ **Recognizes and utilizes personal spiritual gifts?** I am aware of talents and giftings God has given me for the benefit of the larger body of Christ and I willingly use those gifts for God's glory (1 Corinthians 12:7-11; Romans 12:3-8).

Personality and Emotions

_____ **Committed to becoming a well-formed spiritual person?** I seek to leave behind my uncontrolled nature and to demonstrate the presence of the fruit of the Spirit in my attitudes and behavior (Galatians 5:16-23; Colossians 3:5-10).

_____ **Demonstrates the marks of emotional maturity?** I accept responsibility for my own actions. I keep commitments and honor deadlines. I am able to deal with disappointment in others and myself without becoming discouraged and giving up (Matthew 5:37; James 5:12).

_____ **Is able to manage anger in appropriate ways?** I am able to resolve my anger in constructive, non-aggressive ways. I am willing and able to receive criticism graciously and with an open mind. I am able to deal with angry persons in loving and constructive ways (Ephesians 4:26-27; James 1:19-20).

_____ **Demonstrates a positive self-image?** I have a realistic assessment of my strengths and weaknesses. Because of this I am able to express feelings of love, admiration, or praise to other persons and I am able to receive praise and affirmation graciously without embarrassment (Philippians 4:11-13).

_____ **Knows personal limits?** I recognize the limits to my knowledge and ability. I recognize when I am overstressed and know how to cope productively with that stress (2 Timothy 4:9-13).

_____ **Understands the nature and causes of conflict?** I manage my desire to either cause or avoid conflict. I can identify various forms of conflict and their sources. I have practiced some ways to successfully resolve conflict, developing a usable conflict management style (Galatians 2:11-14, 6:1-5).

_____ **Demonstrates a coachable attitude?** I am willing to receive input from others and practice seeking out people who can help me grow. Others see in me a teachable, coachable spirit (2 Timothy 3:10-17).

_____ **Presents an attitude of collegiality?** I work well with others. I am able to share in group processes without being overly passive or overbearing. I don't always need to be in control, thus giving space for others to contribute and lead (Acts 16:6-10).

Personal Matters

_____ **Demonstrates personal care?** I take good care of myself emotionally, physically, and spiritually. In dress and personal habits I present an appearance of Christ to those I meet (2 Peter 3:3-4).

_____ **Understands and is committed to the biblical standard of sexual morality?** I have a healthy, positive attitude toward my own sexuality and (if married) I am able to enjoy a fulfilling sexual relationship with my spouse. I know the power of sexual feelings and I do not underestimate my vulnerability to temptation. I am able to relate to persons of the opposite sex as persons rather than as objects of sexual desire. This includes keeping away from pornography on the internet, in movies, and live performances (1 Corinthians 7:2-7).

_____ **Is faithful to family?** I value my family heritage and honor my parents. (If married) I treat my marriage as the most important human relationship in my life and actively nurture and cultivate it. I practice setting limits on my work in order to be a faithful marriage partner to my spouse and parent to my children (Ephesians 6:2; Hebrews 13:4).

_____ **Presents a lifestyle and quality of life befitting a godly leader?** I practice moderation and health in my eating and physical fitness. I understand the need to balance work, recreation, and rest. I do not abuse tobacco, alcohol or other potentially harmful substances. I am not dependent on chemical substances of any kind (1 Peter 4:12-16; 1 Corinthians 6:18-20).

_____ **Is a good financial steward?** I practice a spirit of contentment that does not depend on material possessions. I live within my means, use credit and credit cards with caution, and avoid financial situations that may compromise my integrity. I pay my taxes as required by law (Matthew 7:19-21, 22:20-22).

_____ **Has a good reputation in the community outside the church and is involved in community affairs?** I try to maintain positive relationships with people in my community. I protect the integrity of my reputation (1 Timothy 3:7; 1 Peter 2:11-17).

_____ **Protects relationships with others?** I am not prone to gossip and I can keep confidences others share with me (Psalm 34:13; Ephesians 4:25).

Leadership Skills

_____ **Is able to be a leader?** I perceive myself as a godly leader and others typically look to me for direction and leadership. I am able to develop goals, objectives and strategies for the church under the guidance of the Holy Spirit and have the abilities to bring vision to reality (Titus 1:5-9).

_____ **Is able to serve as well as lead?** I serve others graciously (protecting the dignity of those served), discreetly (without need for others to notice), and cheerfully (without complaint). I recognize that I may be tempted to abuse the authority of leadership. I seek to protect and care for persons who are emotionally weak and vulnerable (Ephesians 6:6-8).

_____ **Is able to build a sense of community in the local church?** I understand the church is the family of God and I draw people to involvement with the church as valuable members of the body of Christ. I model Christian love and fellowship in my relationships with people in the local church (1 John 4:7-12; Acts 18:24-26).

_____ **Is able to conceive, prepare, and deliver original, biblically based presentations (sermons, lessons, talks)?** I believe that the Bible speaks to real human needs and that God uses people like me to communicate himself. I am capable of holding people's interest when I speak. Others appreciate and grow when I speak or teach (1 Timothy 4:11-16).

_____ **Demonstrates caring skills for others?** I am able to provide care for others in a variety of contexts: celebrations, crises, hospital visitation, grief ministry and other human needs (1 Timothy 5).

_____ **Is able to plan and lead meaningful worship experiences?** I can speak, pray and read the Bible in public. I understand the special emphasis placed on worship as the gathering of the community of faith around the Lord's table and the word of God. I can plan and lead a worship experience that integrates songs, readings, and a sermon or lesson around a common theme (1 Timothy 2).

_____ **Is a competent administrator?** I manage my time and others' time effectively. I am able to prepare an agenda and chair at meetings, including keeping accurate records. I can develop long-range plans and maintain a church calendar. I can write effective letters, memos, reports and other communications so people can understand them easily (Romans 12:3-8).

_____ **Understands structures and systems?** I understand the way things get done. I see areas of need and can devise ways those can be met consistently and appropriately (Acts 6:1-7; 1 Timothy 5:3-11).

Missional Leader Thinking

_____ **Has a vision for church growth?** I understand the difference between maintenance ministry and growth ministry. I am able to describe my philosophy of evangelism and outreach. I practice sharing my faith with others and have led others to a faith decision in Jesus shown in baptism. I am able to cope with resistance to church growth in ways that do not make people feel threatened or defensive (Acts 9:15-16; Romans 15:15-16).

_____ **Is committed to leading the church to accept the mission of God in our nation and to the world?** I believe that new churches are the most effective way to reach more new people for Jesus. We should plant new churches in our own community, in our nation, and in the nations of the world. I am able to build support for the mission of God that leads our church to commit resources to spread the Gospel (Romans 15:20; Matthew 28:18-20).

_____ **Is able to help the church see the world through God's eyes?** I understand the biblical principles of love, justice, and responsibility for our neighbors as a foundation for Christian social responsibility. I am able to lead people in understanding and practicing faithful stewardship of God's creation (Genesis 19-20).

Reporting

Record your scores on page 5 of your personal answer book and answer the associated question.

Record your scores here. How many of each letter did you have?

_____ **E** - Excellent

_____ **S** - Satisfactory

_____ **US** - UnSatisfactory

_____ **UC** - UnCertain

From your answers above, what is the area in which you feel you have made the most progress as a Christian leader? How did you make this progress?

_____
_____
_____
_____

From your answers above, what is the area to which you need to give the most attention? How might you do this?

_____
_____
_____
_____

Talk through this inventory with your spouse. What insights does she or he have for you? What plans can you pursue together to help you mature as a missional leader?

_____
_____
_____
_____
_____
_____
_____
_____

Unit B
Your Walk With God

Lesson 4: Developing Spiritual Habits

"God makes leaders" is an insightful way to view what God is doing in your life. In his book *The Making of a Leader*, Robert J. Clinton, professor of leadership at Fuller Theological Seminary, sets forth a powerful leadership principle: "Effective leaders increasingly perceive their ministries in terms of a lifetime perspective."[1]

We expect that you are a newer leader, new in faith in Jesus, or are coming into ministry from a secular job. No matter your situation, God has you on an amazing growth curve! We believe that God can, will, and does use everything in your life to form you into the kind of leader whose life is a glory to him.

When we speak about a lifewalk with God, what we're saying is that people choose a path, a specific path, on which to do life. When you made the choice to follow Jesus, you chose his path. In one sense, you chose to give up your "right" to make all of your own decisions and gave Jesus that right. When you said, "Jesus is my Lord," you said there are a lot of other paths available to you that you're not going to take. I think this may be one of the better ways to understand the meaning of Jesus' teaching about narrow paths and gates in Matthew 7:13.

In this unit, you will plan your daily time with God, engage a prayer team on your behalf, and consider how far you have come in your life's journey with God.

Reading: Barton chapters 5-6

Barton writes about the leader's fatal question, the question that, when answered, takes you on a journey from which you cannot turn back. Leadership is a weighty lifestyle. Leaders carry responsibility. That responsibility is the care of others, sometimes when they have no care for themselves. It is this weight of responsibility that often drives leaders away from leadership. It seems easier to just take care of ourselves and let others do whatever they want.

Barton's answer to the leadership dilemma of weighty responsibility is the practice of silence. I love her quote about solitude as the place where "we argue out our ambivalence about our calling to leadership openly with God so that it doesn't leak out and create uncertainty in those we are serving." (Barton, p. 81)

---

1. Robert J. Clinton, *The Making of a Leader* (Colorado Springs, CO: NavPress, 1988), 22.

Our solitude is not, however, the end game; solitude that is genuine results in outward action. In chapter 6 Barton opens the road map of the spiritual journey for us. It's not a straight line. In the same way the people of Israel wandered through the desert, so we also find ourselves wandering along our lifewalk with God. The secret for godly leadership is that we know what the journey is like. That's why we can lead others upon it.

The Daily Office

The Daily Office is an historical Christian practice of time with God. It is sometimes referred to as the Liturgy of the Hours. As early as 200 AD Tertullian (c. 160 – c. 220 AD), bishop of Carthage in North Africa, encouraged Christians to pray at the third, the sixth and the ninth hours of the day, thus the reference to "the Hours."[2] By the fourth century AD, these daily times of prayer, song, and reflection on scripture were firmly established in the monastic tradition of both the Eastern Orthodox and the Western Catholic churches.

You may have tried off and on to do a daily quiet time. If you're like me and many people I know, you dropped in and out of your practice, holding on by your fingernails when you were doing well and feeling guilty when you weren't. Yet you have that nagging sense of "I really need this." You're right! You do need it. Robert Mulholland says this: "If we are to engage the deeper journey into Christlikeness, if we are going to become more consistent in the integration of our personal and public intimacy with God, we must commit ourselves to a daily office."[3]

The purpose of the Daily Office is to give you time and place to engage your journey into the heart of God. It's a spiritual law that when you don't go on your spiritual journey neither will those you seek to lead.

Practice the Daily Office

Following is an explanation of how to practice the Daily Office. Mulholland suggests a six element Office. Imagine you are entering into your own private office situated deep within God's heart.

Sit in the Chair. The chair is your meeting place with God. This is *your* chair. It is made for you, supplied by God as the place where you and he meet. As you settle yourself into your chair, your purpose is to center yourself in God's presence. Sit, take a few deep, cleansing breaths. Close your eyes and allow your mind to empty for a moment. Take another deep breath and request God to let you join his presence. Mulholland suggests you find a phrase that you can recite daily, such as, "God, your love is new every morning. Let me join you today in your activity in my life and your world for newness of life."

2. Tertullian, *On Prayer*, 25.
3. M. Robert Mulholland, *The Deeper Journey* (Downers Grove, IL: InterVarsity, 2006), 159.

Look out the Window. The window is your view of the world from your particular vantage point. Your desire is to experience God as the primary reality of your world. As you look out your window, look out upon the landscape of your day. What do you see? What challenges, events, and people are facing you today? Let God show you what your day could look like if you let him have his way in it. "Father, let me join you today in these activities. Point me to your ways and let me follow your lead."

Turn on the Light. The light is the presence of God's glory with you. One of the saddest pieces of scripture is John 1 where John speaks of Jesus as the light of the world, a light that people refuse to see. As you turn on the light of your office, you are letting God shine his light into your life. Ask him to reveal those places where you place caring for yourself as more important than God. As you go through your day and find yourself caring more for yourself than God, tell God, "I love you more than this," and let that thing go.

Let go the Phone. The phone represents everything that keeps you from God. Cell phones, e-mail, and text messages truly make ours a 24/7 world. Nothing ever turns off. When you go to sleep or take the weekend off, you know the next time you turn on the phone or computer you will face a stack of demands. The temptation is to let those demands become your controlling influence. Let go the phone! Abandon yourself to God. This is your prayer time. Give him the attention your other communication usually demands. Listen for his response. Respond to what he says.

Open the Book. The book is God speaking his word to you. There are many ways to approach your Bible reading. You might use a chronological Bible through the year or a daily Bible reading guide. My friend Gary Rohrmayer will study a Bible character or book for a year. He will read the top recommended books as he reads along with the biblical text. I find myself enjoying a variety of reading forms. In recent years I have read through Psalms while giving each a one or two word title and read through the historical books of the Old Testament, identifying short, succinct leadership lessons, which I then tweeted. One year my son-in-law challenged me to read through the New Testament in Greek with his graduate school class. The idea is to be creative and tailor your reading to supply the needs of the season of your life. While not mandatory, I encourage you to keep a reading record of some kind. Record each day what you read along with the insights God gives you.

Do Not Disturb. Finally, end your Office with some moments to sit in silence and stillness. Our lives are filled with so much white noise, much from outside us and some from inside. My wife, a nurse practitioner, speaks about the importance of children learning to settle themselves. This is the skill that allows them to be peaceful in the world. People who fail to learn to settle become so frantic, so overwhelmed with life,

> SPEND SOME TIME WITH GOD EACH DAY SO HE CAN MINISTER TO YOU

that they become physically and emotionally hyperactivated. When you sit in silence and stillness you settle yourself in God's presence. "Be still and know that I am God" (Psalm 46:10).

You can accomplish all six of these steps in as little as ten minutes a day. Your purpose is to spend some quality time with God each day so he can minister to your soul. Are you ready? There's no better time to begin than right now.

For the next three months, practice the Daily Office five days each week. This gives you two days a week to miss, but perhaps after a time of practice, missing will be exactly how you will feel. Check off the days you practice the Daily Office on the calendar on page 6 of your personal answer book.

Practice the Daily Office for a week, then answer the questions below.

What did you learn about yourself as you kept your Daily Office? Was it easy or hard? Did you notice any patterns that prevented you from keeping your Daily Office?

___

What did you learn about God as you kept your Daily Office? Was God accessible for you?

___

Lesson 5: Leading With Prayer

By Acts 12, life had become dangerous for Jesus' apostles. Peter and John had been hauled before the Sanhedrin Council (Acts 4). Stephen had been killed (Acts 7). A persecution against the church swept through Jerusalem, severe enough that many public leaders and preachers left Jerusalem for the rural areas of Palestine (Acts 8). Acts 12 begins with James, the twin brother of John, being killed by Herod Agrippa I who sensed political gain could be bought with the apostle's blood. With the mob hungry for more, Herod arrested Peter.

What do you do when your life is at risk, when the world is crashing down upon you? Peter didn't do much. He was locked up, incommunicado. But notice verse 5. "So Peter was kept in prison, but the church was earnestly praying to God for him." We could think the church responded in prayer because this was all it could do. I rather think this has it backwards. The church didn't start praying because Peter was arrested. No, what the church did was to turn its already activated prayer focus onto Peter. This prayer focus was not new; these Christians were already prayer veterans, skilled and practiced in the art of spiritual intercession.

Prayer is the essence of the Christian's involvement with the world. J. Hudson Taylor, missionary founder of the China Inland Mission said, "The prayer power has never been tried to its full capacity. If we want to see mighty wonders of divine power and grace wrought in the place of weakness, failure and disappointment, let us answer God's standing challenge, 'Call unto me, and I will answer thee, and show thee great and mighty things which thou knowest not!'"

Hudson Taylor

For the godly leader, prayer must be not only a personal practice; godly leaders must learn how to cover themselves in prayer as they engage the spiritual forces of the world. You see, Christian leadership is not just leadership practiced as a Christian. Christian leadership is the practice of spiritual warfare as we seek to loosen Satan's grip on the world so that, as Jesus said, "the gates of Hell will not prevail" (Matthew 16:18).

Organize a Prayer Team

Have you ever led a team of people to pray specifically for you for a season, a purpose, or even simply because you knew you needed prayer intercession in order to accomplish the tasks God had set before you? Most Christian leaders have not. This lesson has somehow been lost to many of us. There are several levels at which to organize a prayer team, depending on your team's purpose.

Prayer of the Multitudes

The broadest level of invitation to prayer is to the multitudes. You invite everyone you know in as broad a way as possible. This forms a prayer team of strangers and usually is for a specific reason or short-term purpose. A prayer request to the multitudes is general in nature, such as, "Pray for our mission trip and that people will respond to Jesus." You don't typically share sensitive or highly personal information to the multitudes because this size prayer group exists in the public realm.

Prayer of the Group

The mid-size invitation is to a group. Often this group already exists. It may be a Bible class or a small group at a church. It may be a group of friends or a club. Prayers asked at the group level can be more personal because you know these people and they know you. "I've been fighting malaria the past few weeks and it has really worn me down. Pray that not only will I get over this bout, but that God will protect me from more sickness." You share things with some sense of confidentiality tempered by the knowledge those prayer items may be shared beyond the group to those who don't know you or the situation well.

Prayer of the Band

The most personal prayer team is the small, intimate group. It's "the band of brothers" idea popularized in the 2001 HBO movie about a squad in the 82nd airborne during World War II. These are people whom you know deeply, with whom you have shared life and who are all for you. This is usually a small number of people at any one time, perhaps three or four close friends, people who have mentored you, or church leaders whom you respect and desire to gain their prayer focus on your behalf. With the intimate prayer band, you should feel comfortable to share the deeply personal issues of life, trusting that these people will hold those things in confidence. "I am really hurt by the things so-and-so has said. I am angry and resentful and I don't know how to deal with this situation."

Action Step

Your assignment is to organize and lead a small, intimate prayer team at the band level to pray for you as you work through this module of the Emerging Leader Training series. You will ask these people to be involved in specific prayer.

1. Lead your prayer team to pray for you weekly. You may think they will do this easily, but they probably will not. Many of God's people have lost the habit of consistent intercessory prayer. As a leader, your role is to influence your team back into the habit of prayer. Do this by:

- Having weekly personal prayer time with one individual on your prayer team, either in person or over the phone. If people have not prayed over the phone before, they may feel uncomfortable with this practice at first. Encourage one another in this type of distant prayer and you may find it very enjoyable.

- Send a weekly e-mail or text message update to your team that they can use to pray for you.

- For bigger prayer items or those that are heart level, call your prayer team to meet together. If God answers a prayer in an obvious way, call your team together to celebrate! Eat ice cream. Throw a party. Do something significant to celebrate God's activity.

2. Lead your team to pray for your church's passion for God's lost people in your community. What is the passion level for God's lost people in your church? Do you see the lost in your midst? Do you know who they are? Do the believers in your church talk about lost people? When your church gathers, do people share conversations they have had with lost people about faith, Jesus and God's love for lost people? Do you hear public prayers for God's lost people in your gatherings? How often we assume a passion, only to find that our church's passion for lost people barely registers. Your prayer team will be God's force for passion for his lost people in your church.

3. Lead your team to be part of a prayer network for God's lost people in America. At Kairos, our goal is for one thousand people to give ten minutes a month of dedicated prayer for God's lost sons and daughters. We call this the Kairos Prayer Network (kairosprayer.org). Encourage your prayer team to join this prayer network. Encourage them to become a monthly prayer partner for lost people and the new churches that are seeking them. Kairos will send each person on your prayer team a welcome and an invitation to join the prayer network. And don't forget to join this prayer network yourself! By leading your prayer team to engage in a large prayer focus, you are leading them to expand their view of God's kingdom.

4. Share with them your commitment to complete this module and how you hope to grow through the process. As you work through the activities of this module, allow your prayer team to journey with you and be blessed by it.

"THE MAN WHO MOBILIZES THE CHRISTIAN CHURCH TO PRAY WILL MAKE THE GREATEST CONTRIBUTION TO WORLD EVANGELIZATION IN HISTORY."

ANDREW MURRAY

Write your plan for your prayer team here. Complete the prayer team form on page 7 of your personal answer book.

My Personal Prayer Team

These are the people on my prayer team. The prayer team leader's name is circled. (That's right. You are not the leader. Nor is your missional director.)

_____
_____
_____
_____
_____
_____

My plan to communicate with them is:
_____
_____
_____
_____
_____

My prayer team will run from
_____
to
_____

Lesson 6: Considering Your Life

Reading: Barton chapters 7-8

Limits and rhythms. Barton uses these two words to explore the fringes of leadership, the edges of our own personal envelopes of physical, emotional and spiritual capacities. Limits have to do with other words such as speed, pace, amounts, and time. Sometimes we lump all these together under the tyrannical word "busyness."

Rhythms are the healthy solution for our limits. If we are working too hard, we add more time off to our schedule, but this approach soon wears us out, too. Finding rhythm is finding a healthier cadence of life. It's the left that follows the right. It's the time off that sustains the time on. It's the stillness that energizes the action.

Barton challenges you to become a craftsman of life. Your life is the only material you have to work with and you are the only one who can do the work.

Timelines

Timelines are familiar tools. They help us see what happened and when in relationship to other events. Our lives are timelines. When you look back at your life you see the big life stage divisions: childhood, elementary school, high school, young adult life, marriage, child-rearing, etc. On top of these big divisions are your life experiences. Some life experiences are just that—experiences, like memories of vacations or holidays or camping trips. Other experiences are more impacting.

Significant Events

Significant life events change us. It may be an insight someone provides us about ourselves. It could be a word of advice that we practice into an ingrained habit. However these significant experiences come, we consider them important and we remember them.

What are two significant experiences in your life and why were they significant?

1. _____
_____
_____
_____

2. _____
_____
_____

Trajectory Setting Events

A second type of life event is a trajectory setting event. You see your life move in a certain direction because of this kind of event. Examples of trajectory events are learning how to play an instrument that leads you to major in music or a conversation with a significant person who saw potential in you that set you on a career path. It could be the loss of a relationship or a person. Do you see how trajectory events significantly impact you? They are like forks in the road that take you into new directions.

What are two trajectory events you can identify in your life and what new directions did they send you on?

1. _____
_____
_____
_____

2. _____
_____
_____
_____

Decision Points

Finally, you have decision points in your life. If you think of your timeline as a string, your experiences are the string fibers. The trajectories are new strands added in. Decisions are like knots in the string. These are the times when you make deliberate, conscious choices about who you will be and what you will do. Decision points are where you take action.

What are two decision points in your life and how did they impact you?

1. _____
_____
_____
_____

2. _____
_____
_____
_____

What we see, then, is that your timeline is not just a sequence of equal events. Your timeline is a story set around big divisions of time. Within those divisions are experiences, trajectory events and decision points. The perspective for you to work with is that God is using these items to shape your life for his purposes.

A Calling Timeline

Tony Stoltzfus is a Christian coach (coach22.com) who has researched the way God interacts with people in a timeline approach. Tony has blessed us by making his timeline creation material available online. In this activity, you will explore God's calling in your life.

Reporting

The following questions will prepare you to develop your personal calling timeline. These questions are adapted from Tony's workbook, *A Leader's Life Purpose*.[4]

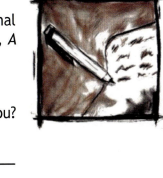

What are two areas of your current life situation that energize you? What two areas of your life drain you?

___
___
___
___
___
___
___

Describe two character qualities that you feel most reflect who you are as a person.

___
___
___
___
___
___
___

---

4. Tony Stoltzfus, *A Leader's Life Purpose* (Virginia Beach, VA: Coach22, 2009), 10-12.

Give an example of a difficult experience or trajectory event you've gone through that has prepared you for a life calling.

_____
_____
_____
_____
_____

What two decisions have you made about your life that have most impacted you? These may be either positive or negative decisions.

1. _____
_____
_____
_____

2. _____
_____
_____
_____

How closely do you feel you are on course with what God has called you to?

_____
_____
_____
_____
_____

Describe one life message—a message you feel God has given you thus far in your life. In other words, what message is God sharing with others through you?

_____
_____
_____
_____
_____

Understanding a Calling Timeline

As you reflect on your life through creating your personal calling timeline, we believe God will make his current calling in your life clearer. If you are a younger leader, you may just be entering your first calling period. As you can guess, a person typically experiences several calling periods across a lifetime. As we age we are able to get a longer, more detailed perspective on what God is doing in us, with us and through us. This life perspective may allow you to see the overall calling that was represented in some way through each of your calling periods. As a younger leader you have the opportunity to be aware of God's intentional activity in your life early so you can anticipate and respond to his next calling in your life.

Reflecting

Tony Stoltzfus has identified a common pattern of growing into God's unique preparation and calling that he incorporates into a personal timeline. Go to Tony's website at thecallingjourney.com and open the timeline builder. Read the introduction to the Calling Journey Timeline to prepare to build your own calling timeline.

First, take some time to look over the Joseph Calling Timeline Tony provides, reproduced here for your convenience. The Calling Timeline is built around a series of hills and valleys. As you read through Tony's descriptions of these hills and valleys, write down your understanding of each of them below. Don't apply your own life to this process yet. That will be your next step. For now, just briefly explain each hill or valley.

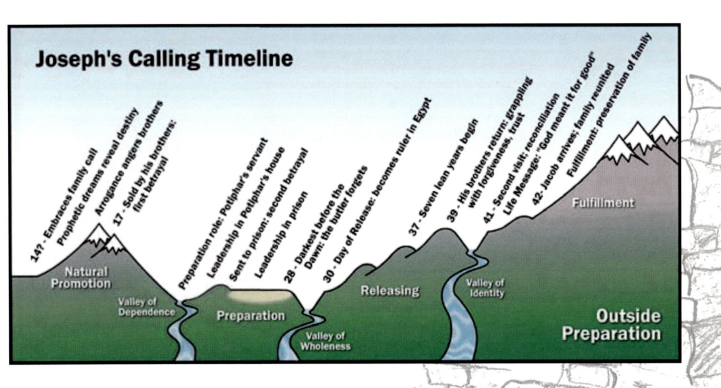

1. Hill of Natural Promotion

_____
_____
_____

2. Valley of Dependence

_____
_____
_____

3. Hill of Preparation

_____
_____
_____

4. Valley of Wholeness

_____
_____
_____

5. Hill of Releasing

_____
_____
_____

6. Valley of Identity

_____
_____
_____

7. Hill of Fulfillment

_____
_____
_____

Your Personal Calling Timeline

Action Step

Follow the website instructions to create your own personal calling timeline. If you are younger, you will reach a point where the questions no longer make sense for you. This means you have reached your current point of personal development. When you reach that point, stop. Save your work and print out your timeline. Print out the graphic overview and tape it to page 8 of your personal answer book.

Reporting

Step back and take a look at your timeline. What do you see? Are there patterns you can observe? What can you learn about yourself? Take a few moments to reflect, and then answer the next few questions.

Describe what you see in your personal calling timeline.

_____
_____
_____
_____
_____

What insights does your calling timeline bring out to you?

_____
_____
_____
_____
_____

As you look at your timeline, name the hill or valley where you are at this moment. Remember, if you are younger, you may not have traveled very far down the calling timeline.

_____
_____
_____
_____

With your timeline in front of you, give your best description of your current calling in life.

_____
_____
_____
_____
_____
_____
_____
_____

Prayer Team

Remember your prayer team. Not only are they covering you with prayer for transformation and courage to continue on this journey, you are providing them encouragement to go on their own spiritual journey. Share something from your timeline with them. Let them know you are listening for and discerning God's call on your life.

What are you learning about team development by organizing and leading your prayer team?

_____
_____
_____
_____
_____
_____
_____
_____

For further reading:

Tony Stoltzfus, *A Leader's Life Purpose*, Virginia Beach, VA: Coach 22, 2009.

Unit C
Your Heart Passions

Lesson 7: Your Heart Passions

God created us emotional beings. We love and hate, we laugh and cry, we enjoy and despise. What is fascinating about our emotions is that they so often direct our choices. Our passions are connected to our motivations; they compel us to action.

The 2006 movie *Amazing Grace* chronicled William Wilberforce's crusade to end slavery in the British Empire. Wilberforce was a member of Parliament when in 1785 he had a sudden conversion to evangelical Christianity. This launched a career marked by a passionate legislative pursuit for social justice. The crown jewel of Wilberforce's career was his anti-slavery crusade. Starting in 1787 Wilberforce spent two years developing his case to introduce an anti-slavery bill in the House of Commons. This culminated in perhaps his most famous speech. On Tuesday, May 12, 1789, Wilberforce concluded his speech before the House with these words:

William Wilberforce

> *As soon as ever I had arrived thus far in my investigation of the slave trade, I confess to you sir, so enormous so dreadful, so irremediable did its wickedness appear that my own mind was completely made up for the abolition. A trade founded in iniquity, and carried on as this was, must be abolished, let the policy be what it might,—let the consequences be what they would, I from this time determined that I would never rest till I had effected its abolition.*

Yet Wilberforce's great speech did not carry the day. It took another eighteen years for the abolition act to become law by Royal Assent. It was not until July 1833 that the Emancipation Bill gained its final Parliamentary ratification. Three days later, on July 29, 1833, William Wilberforce died. The abolition of slavery was the polar star of Wilberforce's political career and his life. It was his life passion.

What God lays on your heart is a matter of great concern and interest. When engaging the passions of your heart, you tap into a powerful, motivating force for your life.

Read the following scriptures and consider the difference serving from the heart makes:

- Proverbs 4:23 – It affects your motivation in serving ... so guard your heart.

- Luke 6:45 – It affects your communication in serving ... so work at putting good in your heart.
- Psalms 20:4; 37:4; Proverbs 3:5-6 – It affects your outcome in serving... so trust your heart to the Lord.

Reading: Barton chapters 9-10

"The leader gets voted off the island." (Barton, p. 139)

If you've watched leaders, you've seen what Barton is talking about. In these chapters Barton will bring you face to face with the loneliness of leadership. Chapter nine deals with the loneliness of suffering. The systematic condition of leading people is that we cause our leaders pain.[1] This is often the reason people either drop out of leadership or refuse to accept leadership in a church context. Barton's solution is not to avoid this pain but to embrace it so we can be effective intercessors.

The second type of loneliness Barton investigates is the loneliness of vision. Leaders are not keepers of the status quo; they are trail blazers. Leaders take people someplace new. It is here, in the face of newness, that people rebel against, refuse and reject the initiatives of leaders. New is, by definition, something different. It is change. This difference, this change, raises the level of discomfort and fear in people, which, in turn, drives their resistance. Yet leaders believe that the new condition to which they are leading people will be better for them and that the people will be better for the journey. One of the natural conditions of leadership is the ability to withstand loneliness.

Your Passion Bulls-eye

Since passions are such a powerful influence in our lives, let's take some time to reflect on the passions of your heart. In Colossians 1:29 Paul writes, "I strenuously contend with all the energy Christ so powerfully works in me." This energy, this passion for his calling, led Paul across the length and breadth of the Roman Empire in order to proclaim the good news of a resurrected Lord.

Identify Your Passions

Tony Stoltzfus[2] suggests using a Life Wheel Assessment to identify and clarify heart passions. Take a look at the Life Wheel below. Here Tony arranges the eight topic areas onto a bulls-eye. Read through the descriptions of each topic and think about causes, ideals or themes that you are passionate about. As you do this, Tony suggests you ask yourself the following questions:

- What causes have I invested in long term? What have I volun-

---
1. The book Barton quotes from, *A Failure of Nerve* by Edwin Friedman, is an excellent leadership study.
2. Stoltzfus, *A Leader's Life Purpose*, 69.

teered for or contributed to over the years?

- What are my soapbox topics? (These are the subjects you consistently bring up with people.)
- What needs tug at my heart and compel me to action?
- What in my life brings my emotions to the surface? What do I see or think of that gets me choked up?
- What am I most excited and joyful about in life? What am I most grieved over?

Action Step

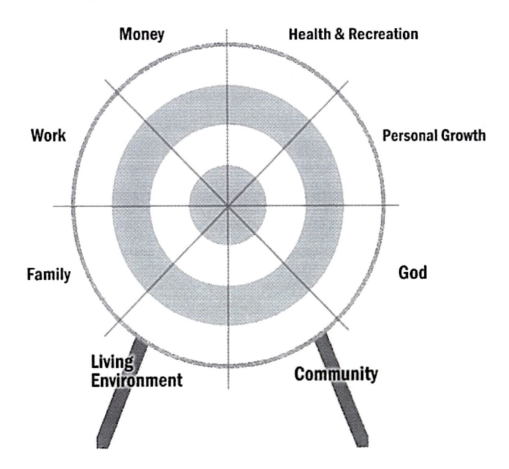

List any passions you may have in each of the eight areas of the Life Wheel. You are not expected to have a passion in every area nor do you need to have three passions for any area. These spaces are provided to spur your thinking.

Work: Your job, career or vocation. (For at home mothers, keeping the family running is your vocation).

a. _____
b. _____
c. _____

Money: Finances, retirement, investments, giving, spending and saving habits.

a. _____

b. _____

c. _____

Living Environment: Your physical surroundings and your things: house, car, yard, photos, furniture.

a. _____

b. _____

c. _____

Personal Growth: What you do to develop yourself: education, training, learning projects, reading—anything that expands your world and develops new abilities or skills.

a. _____

b. _____

c. _____

Health and Recreation: Hobbies, sports, fitness, diet, music, vacations, etc.—the things that take care of your mind, body and emotional health.

a. _____

b. _____

c. _____

Community: Relationship with friends, neighbors and family including political involvement, volunteering, service projects, etc.

a. _____

b. _____

c. _____

Family: Your spouse, children and extended family.

a. _____

b. _____

c. _____

God: Your personal relationship with God plus involvement in religious activities: worship, church meetings, devotions, leadership roles, spiritual disciples, etc.

a. _____

b. _____

c. _____

Read through the passions you uncovered above. What would you pick as your top ten, your strongest passions? Circle them above, then list them below, from one to ten, starting with the most important.

1. _____
2. _____
3. _____
4. _____
5. _____
6. _____
7. _____
8. _____
9. _____
10. _____

On page 9 in your personal answer book, place your current top ten passions onto the bulls-eye by writing the number of each passion in the pie slice of the area of that passion. Place your top two passions in the center bulls-eye circle. Place your third and fourth choice passions in the inner white circle, your passions five, six and seven in the outer dark circle and your final three passions in the outer white circle.

What do you see when you look at your passions displayed on the Life Wheel? Is there a pattern to your passions? Do they tend to group in certain areas? Are there obvious gaps?

_____
_____
_____
_____

5. How do you feel about the way your passions are displayed? If you were to rearrange them, what changes would you make?

_____
_____
_____
_____

Changing Passions

When we take time to observe people, to listen to them, it becomes obvious that each of us has a different and somewhat unique set of passions. This is great. It gives our world variety. Where do our passions come from? How do we develop our passion set? Can we change our passion set, adding new passions and letting go of previously held passions?

The answer is certainly yes. Our passions do change across our lives and, yes, it is possible to deliberately promote changes in our passion sets. Let's open this up a bit. We acquire life passions in five different ways: experiences, exposure, other people, major events, and the action of the Spirit of God.

- **Experiences.** Have you gone on a mission trip to an inner city or a third world country? What did this trip do to you? Sometimes these types of experiences produce dramatic changes in people's passions. I know an elder in a church who made a trip to Russia almost twenty years ago. Since then he has made numerous trips teaching Bible, training leaders and working with orphanages. The Russian people became a passion for him because of an experience. Sometimes you can plan a trip or experience anticipating a passion change. Other times you simply respond to an opportunity and God uses it for his purposes in your life. Be open and aware to the possibility of experiences changing your passion set.

- **Exposure.** Sometimes we develop passions because we are exposed to a new idea or situation through something we read, see or hear about. In 2003 three young filmmakers traveled to Uganda looking for a story. They ended up in the northern frontier town of Gulu where they documented the children soldiers exploited by the Lord's Resistance Army. Since then millions of people have seen and heard about this once invisible tragedy through the Invisible Children Foundation's films and events. Passions can be learned by exposure.

- **People.** Other people's passions can be contagious. When someone you know becomes passionate about a cause or an idea, it influences you. If it means so much to them it calls you to consider the idea too.

- **Major events.** Highly emotional events, personal or world events, are fertile grounds for new passions. In 1999, Pam Cope's son Jantsen died of a heart ailment at age fifteen. Seeking some outlet for the pain of her loss, Pam traveled with a friend to visit orphanages in Vietnam. Out of her pain and that trip, Pam began the Touch A Life Foundation. You can read the story of her new life passion in her book *Jantsen's Gift*.

- **Activity of the Spirit.** Hebrews 4:12 says, "For the word of God is alive and active. Sharper than any double-edged sword, it penetrates even to dividing soul and spirit, joints and marrow; it judges the thoughts and attitudes of the heart." So often we confine this idea to the Bible being akin to a spiritual x-ray machine; it looks inside us to find the sin spots. But what if the word of God is also a planting mechanism, embedding within us the seeds of God's passions that call us towards his desires in our hearts? God can use his word to gift us with new passions that draw us more deeply into his cause.

Action Step

Rewrite your top-ten passion list here. Beside each passion, identify how it originated as well as you can. Use the five ways passions arise listed above. Try to identify how your current passions arose in you.

Passion	Origin

1. _____
2. _____
3. _____
4. _____
5. _____
6. _____
7. _____
8. _____
9. _____
10. _____

Do you sense any new passions growing in you? What might those be? What do you think God may be doing in you at this stage in your life?

_____
_____
_____
_____
_____
_____
_____
_____
_____
_____
_____
_____

Lesson 8: Protect Your Health

Reading: Barton chapters 11-13

One of the most significant principles of biblical leadership is that leadership is best done in a community of leaders. The kings had their counselors. Elders are spoken of in plurals. Leadership communities provide accountability for one another and discernment about what God is doing around them. As you finish reading *Strengthening the Soul of Your Leadership*, engage in the re-envisioning process that Barton lays out. Commit yourself to the type of biblical leadership that honors God, transforms God's people, and takes you to the place of healthy, lifelong leadership. If you are struggling with the commitment, what is getting in your way?

Protect Your Physical Health

Being a spiritual leader is a demanding role, whether you practice ministry as a vocation or as a leader who volunteers your service to God's people. Spiritual leaders have become increasingly susceptible to burnout. Some of the causes for burnout include: the disparity between (somewhat idealistic) expectations and hard realities; lack of clearly defined expectations of ministry; feeling incompetent or unworthy to lead others; internal conflict between being a leader and servant at the same time. Oftentimes people active in intense or longer-term ministry find themselves experiencing burnout. This burnout may have an emotional/physical impact on our lives. Common physical symptoms associated with work burnout are stomach acid and sleep problems. Emotionally, burnout is often symptomized by anxiety, anger and depression.

Just like you can experience work burnout, as a church leader you can also experience spiritual burnout. Spiritual burnout has telltale signs as well. Here's a list of symptoms often associated with spiritual burnout:

- Spiritual apathy or boredom.
- Cynicism.
- Lack of joy.
- Avoiding activities that call you into the presence of God: prayer, scripture reading, and worship experiences.
- Loss of inspiration. As the song says "My eyes are dry, my heart is cold."
- Feeling overwhelmed by the challenges and events of life.

Wayne Cordeiro, founding pastor of New Hope Christian Fellowship in Honolulu, Hawaii, went through a period of work and spiritual burnout. He chronicled that experience in his book *Leading on Empty*. Wayne shares some of his story in a YouTube video.

Watch it now at: youtube.com/watch?v=lnHnq8883ql.

Have you ever had an experience similar to Wayne's? If you have, what were the circumstances that led up to that time? What were your physical and emotional symptoms? What did you do to restore yourself to a healthier place?

In this section, you are developing tools to help you practice Christian leadership and ministry for a lifetime. Taking care of yourself as a Christian leader requires gaining insight into your own character and life. Since stress is a part of life, you cannot ignore it. Rather, pay attention to how you deal with stress.

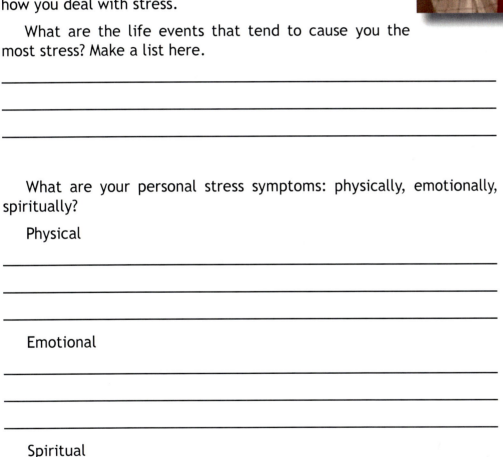

What are the life events that tend to cause you the most stress? Make a list here.

_____
_____
_____

What are your personal stress symptoms: physically, emotionally, spiritually?

Physical

_____
_____
_____

Emotional

_____
_____
_____

Spiritual

_____
_____
_____

We must face it—Satan uses our stress points to tempt us into sin. When we're stressed, our bodies weaken—and so do our spirits and our resolve. For some people stress may result in yelling, sulking, or even physical abuse. Abusing drugs or alcohol may be triggered by stress. Some people seek stress relief through pornography. Church leaders are as tempted by pornography as everyone else. Consider these statistics:

- 51% of pastors said internet pornography is a possible temptation for them.
- 37% of pastors said pornography is a current struggle.
- 75% of pastors do not have any accountability practices for their internet use.[3]

Stress may also lead to what some would consider more benign forms of stress release, such as: watching television, internet surfing, plugging into an iPod, or overspending. These behaviors may not be identified as "sin" issues, yet over time or through repeated indulgence, these actions can have a debilitating effect on our lives. At such points sin does creep in and Satan does his number on us. The way you cope with stress in your life is an important spiritual skill and discipline.

What behaviors are stress induced in your life? Are they harming your health (physical, emotional, and spiritual)? If you're married, talk with your spouse about them. As you feel able, describe some of those behaviors here and how they have negatively impacted your health.

_____
_____
_____
_____
_____

When habits and responses to stress produce hurt in your life, you need to do something about them. This is an act of intervention. Intervention is a process that short-circuits or reorders destructive or debilitating behaviors, replacing them with healthy, constructive behaviors. Here's a simple, five-step intervention process:

- **Name the issue.** This includes the willingness to admit a problem and articulating the problem to a significant other person or people in your life. This is what happens at every Alcoholics Anonymous meeting when someone stands and says, "My name is So-and-So. I'm an alcoholic." When you are able to name and claim the problem, the power that problem has over you decreases. It's a matter of letting light shine into darkness (1 John 1:5-10).
- **Explore the causes.** What is it that is causing the stress? Don't

---

3. "The Leadership Survey on Pastors and Internet Pornography," *Christianity Today* (January 1, 2001): http://www.christianitytoday.com/le/2001/winter/12.89.html?start=2.

just look at the surface causes like, "I don't have enough money," or "I don't like the people I work with." Look for deeper, more personal causes that may be in play (1 John 2:16-17). It may be true that you do not have enough money, but is there an underlying cause, such as desiring to live at the scale of someone else? If so, perhaps there is a seed of jealousy or misfocused ambition at work in you.

- **Assess current coping behaviors.** The reason you have developed these behaviors to stress is that they scratch the itch. On some emotional level they make you feel better. If you're trying to root out or replace a harmful stress behavior, understand why it feels good.

- **Generate alternative behaviors.** Make a plan. It's not enough to say, "I just won't do it again." Think through alternatives and pre-vision in your mind how you will respond in that healthier, more self and God honoring way. The alternative behaviors become your escape route.

- **Develop accountability.** There are few things in the world as powerful as another person to whom you have given permission to ask, "How are you doing with … ?" Don't leave this up to chance. Make a plan. Who will this be? It could be your spouse, a friend, a mentor, or someone else you respect and trust. How often will you contact them? When? Where?

Are any stress induced behaviors harming you, your relationships ,and/or your spiritual walk with God? If so, consider what kind of intervention you need to engage to receive God's victory in this area. As you feel comfortable, choose something you want to work on and plan your intervention here. Remember that the only people who will read this notebook or know what you have written here are those to whom you give permission.

a. Name the behavior:

_____

_____

b. Explore the causes:

_____

_____

_____

_____

_____

c. Assess your coping behaviors:

d. Generate potential alternatives:

e. Develop an accountability plan:

Protect Your Integrity

Our stress reactions are deeply connected to our integrity. Integrity has been said to describe what you do when you are alone. That's helpful, yet integrity is more substantive than this. Godly integrity is imbibing God's nature, his character, into our lives then living out that nature. Paul speaks about this process in this way:

"Therefore, as God's chosen people, holy and dearly loved, clothe yourselves with compassion, kindness, humility, gentleness and patience … Let the peace of Christ rule in your hearts, since as members of one body you were called to peace. And be thankful" (Colossians 3:15-16).

Protecting your character and integrity is critical for a godly leader. Linda Oxford is a good friend and skilled crisis manager for churches. Linda shared with me that eighty percent of negative behaviors that destroy godly leaders may be prevented by making a specific, public commitment to protecting integrity.

Kairos has developed what we call the Ethical Conduct Agreement for ourselves and the planters with whom we work. Once a year each Kairos staff person and planter is asked to publicly read and sign this document in front of others to whom they are accountable. We encourage taking pictures and posting them as a reminder of this important event.

Action Step

Turn to page 10 in your personal answer book and look at the Kairos Ethical Conduct Agreement. Arrange your own ceremony for reading and signing this document in front of others. The Ethical Conduct Agreement is reproduced on the next page.

Ethical Conduct Agreement

"As a minister, I am an ambassador of God and his kingdom. To be a respected representative, I will conduct myself both publicly and privately with the highest degree of integrity and honesty. I will conduct myself in a manner consistent with kingdom values.

"I will treat my wife as Christ treats his bride.

"I will be compassionate, patient and merciful as a parent, giving my children honor and respect. I will not be abusive, neglectful and controlling. I will provide a safe and secure environment for emotional health. I will nurture our relationship and intimacy.

"I will speak as one who has been with Jesus—full of grace and truth. I will guard against sarcastic, caustic and cynical language. I will preach Jesus and the kingdom of God.

"I will take seriously my responsibility to use my power and influence to advocate for the needs of the "least of these"—the children, the poor, the oppressed and other vulnerable others, and to guard them from exploitation, neglect and abuse.

"I will guard myself from obvious sexual temptations with others, in my use of the internet and with other media.

"I will live appropriately in my financial dealings: with my family, my church and with those with whom I do business. I will not use my position or authority for personal gain or benefit.

"I will respect the privileges afforded me through the gifts of churches and Christians. I will treat with respect the equipment, resources and facilities provided me.

"I will work well, making wise use of my time and energies so as to serve the community as a minister of reconciliation for Jesus Christ.

"I accept responsibility for my actions, public and private. I will not become a party to conduct that brings disrespect to me, to fellow Christians or to the greater kingdom of God. I will not tolerate unethical or dishonorable conduct by those connected to me or this ministry."

How did you feel during this ceremony? I'm sure you read the Ethical Conduct Agreement beforehand. Did reading those words aloud in front of your witnesses have a different impact on you than reading them to yourself? In what way?

_____
_____
_____
_____
_____
_____
_____
_____
_____
_____
_____
_____
_____
_____
_____

Prayer Team

Share something you have learned about your passions, your health, or your integrity with your prayer team. How are you helping your team become more involved in God's activity in your life?

_____
_____
_____
_____
_____
_____
_____
_____
_____

Unit D
Your Personality

You are a uniquely made person. God has given you your own personality, background and experiences which he has used to mold you into the type of person he intends for you to be. Uniqueness is part of being human. The combination of personality, background, and experiences that make up your life are unique to you. Rejoice and be glad in them!

At the same time, a commonality exists among us human beings. Have you ever taken a personality inventory, like the Myers-Briggs? It's uncanny how accurate these tools can be in describing us. They describe our strengths and preferences, our weaknesses, and the areas in which we struggle. Ouch! Are we really that predictable? Maybe. Type theory is a way to make sense of and engage with other people based on a few basic, observable preferences and orientations.[1]

In this section you will look deeper into your personality. As you do so, remember that every personality is one of God's gifts to the world. Wouldn't it be boring—and frustrating—if we all shared the same personality? Each personality type brings with it strengths that we enjoy and growth areas that challenge us. Whatever you discover about yourself, be thankful to God for how he has made you.

Lesson 9: Your Personality— The Golden/MBTI

Reading: Peterson, Introduction

When you read Peterson's introduction you may find yourself agreeing with him, or you may wonder why I chose this book for you to read. There is high emotion and even personal indignation in his writing. I think Peterson lets himself go at the beginning so we, his readers, will understand that what he will tell us arises out of the passions of his heart.

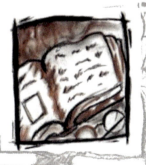

But why all the emotion? Because Peterson will lead you into what he calls the aescetical practices of Christian leadership. Think "running laps, stomach crunches and push-ups." In *Working the Angles*, Peterson introduces you to what he considers the spiritual training regimen of Christian leaders: prayer, scripture reading, and spiritual guidance.

"Woe to me!" I cried." I am ruined! For I am a man of unclean lips, and I live among a people of unclean lips, and my eyes have seen the

---
1. Isabel Briggs Myers, et al., *MBTI Manual, 3rd edition* (Mountain View, CA, 2003).

King, the Lord Almighty."

Then one of the seraphs flew to me with a live coal in his hand, which he had taken with tongs from the altar. With it he touched my mouth and said, "See, this has touched your lips; your guilt is taken away and your sin atoned for."

Then I heard the voice of the Lord saying, "Whom shall I send? And who will go for us?" And I said, "Here am I. Send me!"

Isaiah 6:5-8 TNIV

This is not the flashy stuff that happens in public. It is the disciplined activity that forms the internal life of God's person, the private work that makes this person capable of leading others into God.

The Golden/MBTI

Becoming aware of how God made you is a powerful catalyst to your spiritual growth. The more aware you are of yourself, the better you can respond to God's work in your life. The MBTI is a tool based on highly respected personality theory that has been carefully developed through observation of similarities and differences among a wide sample of people, over many generations and around the world.

One of the inventories at ChurchPlanterProfiles (CPP) is the Golden Personality Type Profiler. The Golden is a Myers-Briggs (MBTI) based instrument. The Golden measures four core personality dimensions that each have two orientations: 1) **E**xtroversion-**I**ntroversion, 2) i**N**tuiting-**S**ensing, 3) **T**hinking-**F**eeling and 4) Organi**Z**ing-**A**dapting (these are Judging-Perceiving in MBTI). According to the MBTI theory we are born with tendencies in each of these dimensions, which mature and congeal over time into a core personality preference which the Golden records as a four letter combination.

Action Step

Log into your CPP account and purchase the upgrade account (the cost is $89 at the time I'm writing this book). This will allow you take the Golden, Portrait Predictor, Leadership 360 and the Spiritual Gifts Inventory. You do not need to do the Strengths Finder.

The Golden and Portrait inventories will take you from thirty minutes to an hour each to complete. The other two won't take as long. Once you pay for and complete these inventories, download the written reports to help you interpret your results.

Reporting

Look through your Golden report and get a feel for the information it gives you.

What are your first impressions as you look at your report? Do you think it is accurate? Does it fit fits you well?

_____
_____
_____
_____
_____
_____
_____

Now look at the table on page 3 of your report. Record your four letter personality type.

_____   _____   _____   _____

The results you received on your Golden are only a hypothesis about your personality. It is important that you go through a verification process with an MBTI certified consultant to confirm your results. Kairos has two certified MBTI consultants on staff who conduct verifications for planters and those on leadership teams. If you do a Kairos Discovery Lab in the future or if your church chooses to participate in a Leadership Team weekend with Kairos in the future you will go through a verification process.

Digging Deeper into the Golden

You now have a four letter type code that suggests a personality type for you. Let's unpack those four letters.

The two middle letters in your personality type code indicate preferences in your cognitive functions. This includes how you take in information (through your **S**enses or through i**N**tuiting) and how you make decisions (through **T**hinking processes or **F**eeling processes).

The final letter in your four-letter type code indicates which of your two cognitive (middle letter) functions you extravert to others, what other notice in you first. If your final letter is an **A**, you extravert how you gather information. This means that you direct your information gathering function (**S** or **N**) toward your outward world so people will most readily see this function. If your final letter is **Z**, you extravert how you make decisions (**T** or **F**). You direct your decision-making function toward the outside world.

Write your four letter Golden type code below and circle your extraverted letter (**S, N, T,** or **F**).

___ ___ ___ ___

Next, let's look at the first letter, the **E** or **I**. These letters, the Extraverted or Introverted, indicate where you focus energy, on what is outside of you or what is inside of you. Extraverts prefer to engage the world around them. Introverts prefer to engage within themselves. These two letters indicate which of your middle two letters is your dominant and which is your secondary function.

Let's do the E first because it is the simplest. If you are an **E** type, your dominant function is the same as your extraverted letter.

But if you are an **I**, the function that you show in an outwardly interactive manner is not your dominant function. If your four-letter type code begins with an **I**, your dominant function is the central letter that you did not circle above. If you circled your Info-gathering function (**S** or **N**) above, then the introverted and dominant function would be the decision-making function (**F** or **T**).

For instance, someone with a personality type of **ESFA** extraverts the Sensing function (the information-gathering function). The dominant function is Sensing, and the secondary function is Feeling. Someone with a personality type of **INTZ** extraverts the Thinking function (the decision-making function). The dominant function is iNtuitive, and the secondary is Thinking. As a result, what this person tends to extravert is not actually what is most valued in his or her life-choices.

In your four letter Golden type code put a square around your dominant function. Remember, if you are an **E** your dominant function will have both a circle and a square around it. If you are an **I**, your dominant function is not the one you circled.

___ ___ ___ ___

Now you have identified with a circle the function you externalize, or show other people. And you have identified with a square your dominant function. Your type code also has a secondary function. This is the middle letter that is not your dominant function. Now you should be able to identify your external, your dominant and your secondary functions.

These concepts may appear complicated at this point. Consider this a brief introduction to these functions. Understanding these processes will become a powerful tool as you develop teams in the next several modules. The concepts will be explained in depth as you progress.

In the space below write your middle two letter combination:

- My middle two letters are: ____ ____
- My dominant factor is: ____
- My external factor is: ____
- My secondary factor is: ____

Personality Type Groups

Here's an insight that the Golden/MBTI provides. David Keirsey[2] used the MBTI designations to describe four basic personality type groupings. We've used the Golden's **Z** and **A** here.

SA - "The Artisans" (light blue). Keirsey describes the SA group's primary objective as "Sensation Seeking." The Artisans prefer jobs where they can troubleshoot, respond to crises and negotiate. They also enjoy identifying and responding to opportunities. The SA grouping includes the types: crafters, composers, promoters, and performers.

NF - "The Idealists" (green). Keirsey describes the **NF** group's primary objective as "Identity Seeking." The idealists enjoy jobs that allow them to support and encourage others. Their tendency to be enthusiastic can energize and improve the morale of others. The **NF** grouping includes the types: healers, counselors, champions and teachers.

ISTA Crafters	ISFA Composers	INFA Healers	INFZ Counselors
The Artisans		The Idealists	
ESTA Promoters	ESFA Performers	ENFA Champions	ENFZ Teachers
ESTZ Supervisors	ESFZ Providers	ENTA Inventors	ENTZ Fieldmarshals
The Guardians		The Rationals	
ISTZ Inspectors	ISFZ Protectors	INTA Architects	INTZ Masterminds

SZ - "The Guardians" (light yellow). Keirsey describes the **SZ** group's primary objective as "Security Seeking." The Guardians prefer jobs that demand responsibility. They enjoy improving the efficiency of processes and setting up standardized procedures. The **SZ** grouping includes the types: supervisors, providers, inspectors, and protectors.

NT - "The Rationals" (red). Keirsey describes the **NT** group's primary objective as "Knowledge Seeking." The Rationals enjoy jobs that demand a high level of expertise and high standards of competence. They enjoy designing and understanding systems. The **NT** grouping includes the types: inventors, field marshals, architects and masterminds.

Among the assets gained in understanding ourselves better is a clearer understanding of others and the way we impact them in our interactions. Extraverts who fill a room with their thinking are sharing themselves rather than ignoring what others think. In teamwork, where

---

2. David Kiersey, *Please Understand Me II: Temperament, Personality, Intelligence, Prometheus Nemesis*, 1998.

the object is to hear everyone's best thinking, this behavior can freeze the process, so for the extravert to benefit from the wisdom of introverts on his team, there might need to be an intentional way of gaining input in a safe/private format like writing, or a smaller grouping. On the other hand, introverts who are motivated to contribute to a team of extraverts need to find ways to be heard.

People who tend to make decisions quickly (**T** and **Z**) are not necessarily reckless. They prefer to move through the information-gathering part of a process quickly so that action can be taken. They might need to have systems in place to be sure they have their facts straight before stepping out. When we understand the strengths and weaknesses of our tendencies, we have a better handle on how to moderate the weaknesses and increase the value of our strengths.

Skills must be mastered to keep our preferences working for us and those who are near us.

Now turn to page 16 of your Golden report. Here you will see a summary of your personality type scores.

What do you see about yourself? To what degree does this fit your own preferences?

_____
_____
_____
_____
_____
_____
_____
_____

Further reading for the Golden/Myers-Briggs:

David Keirsey. *Please Understand Me II*, 1998, www.keirsey.com.

Jane A. G. Kise, David Stark & Sandra Krebs Hirsh. *LifeKeys: Discovery Who You Are*, 2005.

Linda V. Berens & Dario Nardi. *The Sixteen Personality Types: Descriptions for Self-Discovery*, 1999.

Lesson 10: Your Personality—The Portrait Predictor/DiSC

Reading: Peterson, chapters 1-3

These chapters will take you into the heart of academic scholarship. Don't shy away from or be put off by the intellectual argument of a deep thinker. This section contains your most challenging reading assignment for this module. Push through it and let it inform you.

In chapter one Peterson uses the story of the Greek god Prometheus to demonstrate how learning, knowledge, and technology can displace the presence and work of God's divine Spirit in the ministry of godly leaders. He explains how the same scholarly orientation Edward Gibbon used to reinterpret Roman history to make Christianity "the bad guy" was brought into biblical scholarship when Julius Wellhausen stripped the power out of the Psalms, the prayer book of God's people Israel. Later, in a brilliant flash of insight, Sigmund Mowinckel reversed this scholarly conclusion, reinstating the Psalms as the artesian wellspring for prayer in language, content and devotion.

Having firmly restored Psalms as the dynamic center of faith and prayer Peterson takes us into the structure of the Psalter. Psalms was written as five books echoing the five books of the Torah. Where the Torah presents God's creating/saving word to us, the Psalms respond as a believing/obeying reply to God. The Psalter should become our teacher. It teaches us a prayer language that is rich, profound and utterly human.

Finally, in chapter three, Peterson prods us to ingrain the habit of Sabbath into our lives. Yes, the author knows us well. He knows the demands of compassion for people, the never ceasing call of time that masquerades as the essence of work. That's why Peterson reminds us that Sabbath is not a suggestion. It is a command. Nothing less than the command of a God who both knows us and cares for us has enough force to compel us to lay ourselves down in God's presence where he can restore us to our rightful mind and body.

The Portrait Predictor/DiSC

The Portrait Predictor is a DiSC based assessment. The DiSC was developed by Dr. William Marston, a Columbia University psychologist in the 1920s. Where the MBTI is a personality type instrument, the DiSC measures our behavioral preferences or traits. These traits are measures of how we prefer to act in our various environments.

The DiSC is often used in coaching. Steve Ogne and Tim Roehl in their book *TransforMissional Coaching*[3] provide an overview of how the DiSC is useful for more productive coaching relationships.

---

3. Steve Ogne & Tim Roehl. *TransforMissional Coaching* (Nashville: B&H, 2008).

The DiSC based Portrait Predictor measures four primary behavioral styles:

D: Dominant, Driving, Doer

I: Influencing, Inspirational, Impulsive

S: Steady, Stable, Supportive

C: Competent, Cautious, Careful

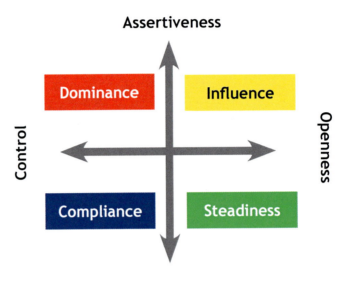

These styles are organized around two axes. The Assertiveness/Receptiveness axis measures the ways in which people react to their environment, specifically whether they take a pro-active or reactive approach. The Openness/Control axis measures a person's social attitudes, describing approaches to interacting with the world. People higher on openness begin with people relationships and work at an emotional level. Those who prefer the control end tend to begin with facts and ideas, preferring rational arguments before emotions.

When these two axes are put together they form a matrix from which the four behavioral styles arise.

Action Step

Download your Portrait Predictor results report from Church Planter Profiles. From page 2 get the following information:

What is your portrait theme from your results report?

_____

What is your descriptor?

_____

Look at page 5 of your Portrait Predictor report, the page with the Team Grid on it. You'll see your star on your descriptor. Notice the explanation. How high or low your star is on the grid indicates your "personal engine speed." People in the top two quadrants prefer a quick pace while people in the lower two quadrants prefer a more deliberate pace. If you are a **D** or an **I**, your engine is more like a sports car. You will tend to work, think and act quickly. If you are an **S** or a **C** your personal engine is more like that of a truck. You don't work as fast but you have a lot of pulling power for the long haul. Both engines are good—they're just different.

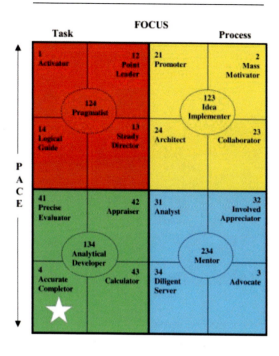

Portrait Predictor Team Grid

Now let's look at the quadrants vertically. People who are in the two left side quadrants prefer to focus on the tasks before them. People who are **D**'s or **C**'s like making lists—and they like marking things off their lists even more! People who are **I**'s or **S**'s tend to focus on processes or systems that will help them accomplish tasks. They're concern is not so much the task, but how they can go about completing it.

The tension points we experience with other people often tend to be between these two axes: pace and focus. Faster paced people get frustrated with slower ones, and vice versa. People who prefer accomplishing tasks get frustrated with those who prefer focussing on processes. This is particularly common in work environments.

Reporting

What are your impressions as you look at your report? Do you think it is accurate? Does it feel like it fits you well?

_____

_____

_____

_____

Turn to page 12 of your personal answer book and record your insights from the Portrait Predictor.

Further reading for the DiSC:

DiSC: discusonline.com

Robert A. Rohm. *Positive Personality Profiles*, 1994.

Missional Director Meeting

Check your calendar on page iv as a reminder that at this point in the module, you should be having your second meeting with your missional director. Adjust the calendar as needed.

Reflecting

God is a creator God (Gen. 1-2) and he doesn't make junk. Your personality, your natural hard-wiring, is God's gifting to you. Your personality type (Myers-Briggs) and your behavioral traits (DiSC) are what you bring to your work, to your marriage and to your church. While your personality temperament is inborn and predisposes you to prefer certain ways of thinking and acting, you are always changing and maturing. As you mature, you will learn how to better use the strengths of your personality, to strengthen your weaknesses, and to broaden your behavioral repertoire until, as David Keirsey says, you "have become a full-blown specimen of what you were meant to be.[4]" Like a tree matures no matter the weather the world brings its way, so you mature through all that life brings your way.

As you investigated your personality through the Golden and Portrait Predictor insight tools how have you come to appreciate your personality?

_____
_____
_____
_____
_____

Given that you are on a path of growth and maturity, what strengths of your personality would you like to employ better and what less developed areas would you like to strengthen in the next year? How will you work with this maturation process to enhance your growth?

_____
_____
_____
_____
_____
_____
_____
_____

---

4. Keirsey, 1998, 22.

Unit E
Your Giftedness

Lesson 11: Thinking Through Giftedness

A number of years ago I read a book that made a lasting impact on my life. It was Gene Edwards' *A Tale of Three Kings: A Study in Brokenness*.[1] Through his sensitive portrayal of three kings of Israel—a king of natural physical attributes (King Saul), a king of deep spiritual reflection (David), and a king of gifted personality but self-absorption (Absalom)—Edwards plows the fields of giftedness with touching sensitivity. Leaders cannot rely soley on their natural giftedness. Edwards' insights changed the texture of my life as he wooed me to reflect on who I am, the way God endowed me with natural abilities, how he equipped me through life experiences, and how he is present in my life through spiritual gifts.

Several years later, as I was working on a masters in leadership at Fuller Theological Seminary's School of World Mission, I took Robert "Bobby" Clinton's class Leadership Emergence Theory.[2] Bobby took us into the depths of the processes through which he identifies God's working in the lives of individuals. I distinctly remember the day he displayed overhead slides (no Power Point in those days) of "portraits" of the giftedness of leaders he and students in his classes had studied. He explained that every person has a giftedness set comprised of natural endowments, acquired skills and spiritual gifts. Bobby gave me a new way to look at my life that, along with the emotional impact of Gene Edwards' book on the kings, has become a constant companion in my spiritual journey.

Reading: Peterson, chapters 4-6

The second angle Peterson addresses is reading scripture. We all do this. Hopefully we do this regularly, even daily. The question Peterson will ask continually in these three chapters is whether we are just reading the word or actually hearing the word—listening to the God who speaks it.

Peterson begins with the idea and process of listening. He builds his case on the principle that words begin as sounds. Here, at this most fundamental point, Peterson asks us to engage the words of scripture as voice because voice is personal. He argues that the words we see and read in the Bible have been, in a sense, sanitized in print form. While every voice is unique with its own voiceprint, written words are neutral-

---

1. Originally published in 1980, you can read the author's "story behind the story" at geneedwards.us.
2. Robert J. Clinton, *Leadership Emergence Theory* (Altadena, CA: Barnabas Resources, 1989).

ized. They are all ink on the page, whether that ink be black or red. The point he makes is that to engage we must be prepared to enter into the dialogue of personal relationship.

Then Peterson looks at the two academic, pastoral skills of exegesis and hermeneutics. Think of exegesis as your personal encounter with the text. In exegesis you encounter the details of the text. The story of Jacob wrestling with the angel is an apt analogy for our exegetical encounter with God in scripture. The reason for exegesis, however, is not just to get the technical specifics (language, word meaning, grammar, etc.). You will know you have spent enough time in the task of exegesis when you begin to hear the accent of God's living voice in whatever context, story or culture he is manifesting himself. Like Lucy in C.S. Lewis's *The Lion, The Witch and The Wardrobe*—you enter through the wardrobe of exegesis into the land where you become part of God's biblical story.

Where exegesis is oriented to the individual, hermeneutics is oriented towards others. In fact, hermeneutics can only occur as we speak meaning from exegesis into the life story of others. Peterson introduces us to a new word to describe this process: *hodegesis*. In *hodegesis* we act as trail-guides. Our goal is to connect with others, to hear their questions, and to guide them in their quest for meaning and understanding.

In this second angle Peterson will challenge you to listen to God, to enter personally into the biblical story and through your personal experience with God in scripture to become a guide for those around you so they can experience the fullness of God as well.

Types of Giftedness

Giftedness is central to a leader's ability to motivate and influence others towards God's intentions for them, with their best interests in mind. One's giftedness also influences what kinds of ministries a leader chooses to do and how he or she will accomplish those ministries. This makes giftedness a key element in leadership development.

In this section you will explore your giftedness set, the collection of natural abilities, acquired skills, and spiritual gifts by which you influence others.

Natural Endowments

Natural endowments are those capacities or abilities a person is born with, such as musical aptitude, physical size or strength, beauty, etc. These endowments cannot be taught, learned, coached or added to. However, they can be harnessed and honed for use in more effective ways.

Michael Phelps, the Olympic swimming phenom, was proclaimed by many to be perhaps the greatest athlete of all time. He won eight gold medals in eight swimming events in Beijing in 2008, shattering seven world records in the process. After adding his medals from the London Olympics of 2012, Phelps has won 22 Olympic medals, 18 of them gold.

Part of Phelps' amazing success is because of his physical endowments. At six feet, four inches tall yet weighing just one hundred and sixty-five pounds, Phelps is long and thin. He has a water predator's body. His immense wingspan of six feet seven inches is normal for someone four inches taller. These extra inches allow him to cover more space than his competitors. His size fourteen feet serve as natural flippers. Plus, his ankles are double-jointed, enabling him to thrust through water as if he's wearing fins. In other words, Michael Phelps is built to swim.

I have a friend who was a competition swimmer at Pepperdine University. My friend loved swimming. He longed to race and had his sights set on qualifying for the US Olympic team. Unfortunately, he was not Michael Phelps. His coach broke his heart one day when he told him, "You just don't have the physical capabilities to be an exceptional swimmer." My friend was a good swimmer because of heart, desire and training. But no matter how many laps he swam or how good the coaching he received, in the end he wasn't built for championship swimming.

Another arena of physical endowment is personality. You've already delved into your personality through the Myers-Briggs. Remember that your personality shows your propensities, your preferred choices for interacting with the world. You may have a propensity that leads you to interact with people. Someone else may be more comfortable dealing internally with ideas. Both are natural endowments, the things you were born with.

Natural endowments propel us in directions we can pursue. They also limit us in other areas. Our endowments are the clay of life. We can shape, form, direct, and mold our clay, but we can never change the composition of our life clay.

> O LORD, YOU ARE OUR FATHER. WE ARE THE CLAY, YOU ARE THE POTTER; WE ARE ALL THE WORK OF YOUR HAND.
>
> ISAIAH 64:8

Action Step

What are Your natural endowments? Take a few moments to reflect on how you were made, what you were born with that has given you direction in your life. Use the three categories below and list some of the natural endowments you see in yourself under each category.

Physical Characteristics	Personality Traits	Mental Abilities

Reflection

As you look at yourself through the characteristics, traits and abilities above, which of them play the biggest part in defining who you are today? How do they do that?

_____
_____
_____
_____
_____
_____
_____
_____
_____
_____
_____
_____
_____

Acquired Skills

Acquired skills are any talents or capabilities which someone learns through practice and application. These may be learned in school, via the internet, from an apprentice or mentor or in other ways. Acquired skills include computer literacy, playing a guitar, learning a foreign language, being a super salesman, skill at Bible study or sharing faith, and many others. Don't forget this area also includes physical activities such as sports, music, and art. A person who is a natural athlete may be able to learn a skill more quickly than one who is not so gifted, but still has to learn the skill in order to use it competently.

Action Step

List some of the skills you acquired in the arenas listed below:

In Your Family	At School	At Work

Reflection

From the list above, which skill, talent, or ability is most enjoyable for you and why?

_____

_____

Which one has been most useful to you and how?

_____

_____

Which one is most fulfilling to you and why?

_____

_____

Lesson 12: Spiritual Gifts

Spiritual gifts are qualitatively different from the endowments and skills we looked at in the last lesson. I consider spiritual gifts to be those God-given capacities, received from the Holy Spirit, that empower the believer to minister over a lifetime or in a momentary situation[3]. Where physical endowments and acquired skills are part of God's natural pathway for human development, spiritual gifts are God's supernatural development process.

Perhaps the clearest example of supernatural gifting for ordinary tasks is found in Exodus 31:1-11. Here God clearly states that he has "given ability to all the skilled workers to make everything I have commanded you." This follows six chapters of detailed instructions on how to build the tabernacle and make its articles, instructions given to people who had been "mud pit" slaves for four hundred years! They didn't have the skill or experience to complete the task God had given them, so he gave them their skill. For subsequent generations we expect that the craftsmanship was passed down normally, master to apprentice, as acquired skill. Sometimes spiritual gifts just appear, other times God energizes what we already have to a new level of use.

SPIRITUAL GIFTS ARE GOD'S SUPERNATURAL DEVELOPMENT PROCESS

Spiritual gifts are also given for a purpose. Paul describes this purpose in 1 Corinthians 12 as "given for the common good (v. 7)," distributed by the Holy Spirit "just as he determines (v. 11)." In the Exodus passage, there was a community need so God provided. In Corinth, there was also community need, so God provided. A question the text does not answer for us is whether these gifts developed over time or were given at peak perfection.

What is interesting about spiritual gifts in terms of leadership is the provision of people gifts. Read 1 Corinthians 12:27-31.

Here Paul associates gifts with people: apostles, prophets, teachers, miracle workers, tongue speakers and interpreters. (See also Ephesians 4:11.) He goes on to describe the function or purpose of these people gifts: "so that the body of Christ may be built up" and gain maturity. God took what already existed in people and turned it into giftings for the benefit of the church body.

Finally, spiritual gifts can be misused and disused. Read 1 Corinthians 14:1-26. Here Paul digs into the misuse of spiritual gifts. In earlier portions of the letter, Paul has already addressed significant spiritual dysfunctions. The contentious spirit Paul addresses in chapter 3 over

---

3. Clinton 1989:411.

who's following the best leader, in chapter 6 over lawsuits pitting one believer against another, in chapter 8 over how to treat food offered to idols, in chapter 11 over head coverings in worship, and abusing others through a distorted practice of the Lord's Supper, is alive and well in these Christians' practice of their spiritual gifts. In other words, just because the gifts are divinely provided doesn't mean they can't be humanly abused. It does not seem farfetched to take 1 Corinthians 14:32 as a directive on the use of all spiritual gifts: "The spirits of prophets are subject to the control of prophets."

The disuse of spiritual giftedness was also a problem. Paul recognized gift disuse in his young protégé, Timothy. In Paul's second letter to Timothy it seems that Timothy ran into a flat spot in his leadership life. Perhaps Timothy was tired, maybe even worn out, and so his spirits and his work were flagging. Paul wrote this letter to Timothy to give him a shot of spiritual 5-Hour ENERGY pick me up. "For this reason I remind you to fan into flame the gift of God, which is in you through the laying on of my hands" (2 Timothy 1:6). Paul doesn't get specific about what Timothy's gift was. Paul's point is that Timothy had let the gift fall into disuse. We can't make a blanket statement, but apparently there is a spiritual principle of "use it or lose it" when it comes to spiritual gifts.

Are spiritual gifts permanent and do they develop over time? This is a question that scripture does not seem to address directly. King Saul, first king of Israel, was given the spirit of prophecy as a sign of his divinely appointed kingship (1 Samuel 10:5-6). The prophetic gift did not seem a permanent gift of Saul's. He certainly did not display that gift later in his reign. My personal experience is that sometimes spiritual gifts are given for a season or a specific purpose. When that season is complete or that purpose has been fulfilled, the gift is no longer needed, so God withdraws it. It also makes sense, especially in regards to people gifts, that experience and use with gifts will hone one's understanding and ability to use those gifts well. Paul certainly expected the Corinthian Christians to mature from misuse to good use of their spiritual gifts, otherwise why would he have spent so much time instructing them?

To summarize this brief study of spiritual gifts:

- Spiritual gifts are given by God, by his Spirit, as the Spirit determines.
- The gifts are given for the common good of the people of God.
- The gifts can be misused and disused.
- Experience suggests that some gifts are given for a season or purpose while others may be permanent.

Identifying your spiritual gifts may not be as straightforward as taking a spiritual gifts test or making an inventory of all the things you're good at, then crowning them as "spiritual gifts." Rather, you need to filter what those tools tell you through the biblical framework we've assembled above to get a sense of your spiritual giftedness.

Action Step

Login to your ChurchPlanterProfiles account and download your spiritual giftedness score sheet. CPP looks at nineteen different spiritual gifts identifiable in scripture. Beside each gift you will see your score for that gift.

Go to page 13 in your personal answer book and graph your gift scores. For example, if your score on Administration is a 15, fill in the boxes on the Administration line up to 15. This will let you see your scores in a visual form.

Reflection

Now, using what you have learned from your spiritual gifts survey and from our discussion on spiritual gifts above, What do you think are your spiritual gifts? List your top five below in order of their strength and importance in your life.

_____
_____
_____
_____
_____
_____

Record your list on page 14 of your answer book.

Just for interesting information, the graphs below show the results of an online spiritual survey tool that looks at giftings for church members (laity) and church leaders (pastors).

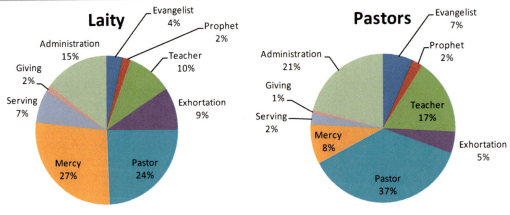

Results from churchgrowth.org, 2004.

Illustrate Your Giftedness Set

Now you're going to draw a picture of yourself. Remember my experience in Bobby Clinton's class when he began showing us "portraits" of leaders' giftedness sets? You're going to draw your own portrait now. Don't panic! You don't have to be artistic to complete this task.

Below is the example of the giftedness set of a leader I studied for a Leadership Emergence Study[4] under Bobby Clinton. Notice the key in the upper left corner. Natural endowments (abilities) are represented by squares, acquired skills by triangles and spiritual gifts by circles. The prominence, strength, and usefulness of a gift is indicated by the graphic's size. The bigger the ability, skill or gift, the bigger the graphic. The interplay of these three types of gifts is represented by their placement. Items that are used together are drawn on top of each other or touching. Other items sit further away. Distance and arrangement among the graphics illustrates the interconnectedness of the gift items. Let's take a closer look at the picture below.

Behailu Abebe is Ethiopian.[5] He was an influential leader during his ministry in Ethiopia. He is now retired and lives in Seattle, Washington. Behailu's giftedness set consists of a complex grouping of these three gift elements, with acquired skills and spiritual gifts as dominant elements. His giftedness set is illustrated below :

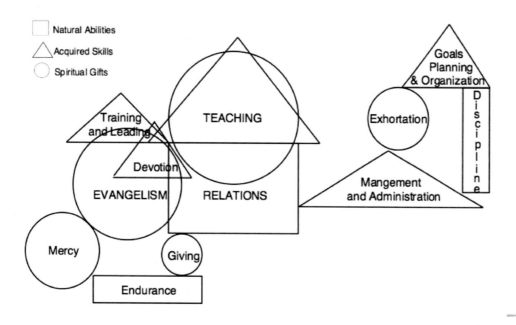

Behailu's giftedness set is distinctive in that it does not have a single focal element, i.e. it is not dominated by one of the three elements of the giftedness set. Both acquired skills and spiritual gifts appear in strength.

---

4. J. Robert Clinton & Richard W. Clinton, *Unlocking Your Giftedness* (Altadena, CA: Barnabas Resources, 1993).

5. Stanley E. Granberg, "Behailu Abebe, Called To Serve: Leadership Emergence in Ethiopia, 1943-1993," unpublished manuscript, 1993.

His dominant grouping of gifts consists of a natural ability in Relations with others, a spiritual gift of Teaching, an acquired skill in Teaching, and the spiritual gift of Evangelism. These are the gifts which were evident throughout Behailu's ministry. They motivated his choice of ministries and the direction in which he moved.

The two spiritual gifts of Mercy and Giving along with the natural ability of Endurance are supportive items in the overall gift-mix. They appeared fairly consistently in Behailu's ministries but were not usually the motivating forces.

The acquired skills of Training and Leading and Devotion are grouped closely with Evangelism. The Training and Leading skill was used mostly in conjunction with maturing and guiding new Christians. The Devotion skill was a fundamental support element which Behailu used to empower his evangelistic and leadership activities. The close association of these skills with the dominant items made them important skills evident in all of Behailu's ministry activities.

The final grouping consists of the acquired skills of Management and Administration and Goals, Planning, and Organizing, the spiritual gift of Exhortation, and the natural ability of Discipline. These items were recurring themes in Behailu's ministry but they were not major motivating items. This group was usually used on an "as needed" basis according to the situation, for example, during the Ethiopian famine relief program of 1984-1985 when the Churches of Christ distributed more than eight million dollars worth of relief goods.

It was interesting to me when Behailu finished creating his giftedness set picture he was so excited. He kept saying, "This is me, it really is me."

Action Step

You are going to create what is called a Venn diagram. A Venn diagram simply uses shapes, shape sizes and spacing to illustrate something visually. You will use the three shapes:

1. Squares represent natural endowments
2. Triangles represent acquired skills
3. Circles represent spiritual gifts

Shape size. This is the easiest to grasp. The more important a gift item is, the bigger you will make the shape that represents it. For example, in Behailu's diagram, his teaching gift is the largest, the most prominent. As you look over your giftedness you will make the most important or most prominent items large and make the less important items smaller.

Spacing. This is a bit more complicated. When you place your gift symbols on the paper think in terms of groups. What items do you seem to use together? These are gift clusters. Place gifts that cluster into a group.

In the diagram to the right, all three gifts overlap some. Sensitivity to People is the most prominent gift, so it is the largest. Mercy overlaps the most with Sensitivity and Listening Skills overlaps a little with both Sensitivity and Mercy.

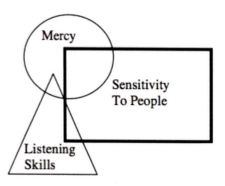

Gift items do not have to touch. If an item is used alone, show it by itself. Or you may have clusters of gifts where gifts within the cluster touch or they may not touch. The more related gift items are the closer they are to each other. The less related they are the further apart you will place them.

Also, you will put the more important gift items or clusters towards the center of your page and those that are more peripheral to the edges.

Here's another example of a leader's giftedness set.

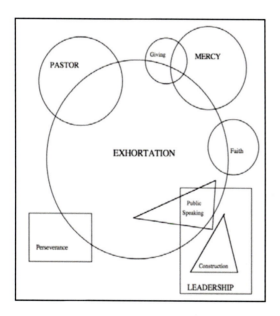

The spiritual gift of Exhortation is the central gift in this leader's set, surrounded by the other gift items.

The spiritual gifts items (circles) are supported by the natural abilities of Perseverance and Leadership.

There is a gift cluster made up of Leadership and the acquired skills of Public Speaking and Construction.

Turn to page 15 of your answer book and draw your personal giftedness set.

Reflecting

What have you learned about yourself and your giftedness?

_____
_____
_____
_____
_____
_____
_____
_____
_____
_____

Prayer Team

Your prayer team is a group of people you are leading. Don't let them flounder. Don't leave them wondering what is happening. A leader must learn to provide resources to his or her teams. You have just completed a study on giftedness. What can you use from this study to resource your prayer team?

_____
_____
_____
_____
_____

Further reading on giftedness

Kenneth Berding, *What Are Spiritual Gifts?* Kregel, 2007.

Christoph Schalk and Jon Haley, *The Three Colors of Your Spirituality*, ChurchSmart Resources, 2001.

Charles F. Stanley, *Ministering Through Spiritual Gifts*, Nelson: Touch Series, 1999.

Unit F Practicing Spiritual Disciplines

Lesson 13: Disciplines and World Engagement

Lilias Trotter (1853-1928) grew up in London in a family of wealth and social standing.[1] By her twenties she developed such skill as an artist that the noted painter and illustrator John Ruskin claimed her to be a significant talent.[2] Yet in 1888, at age thirty-four, inspired by her love for Christ and a devotion to human flourishing Trotter left England for Algeria to organize a mission for the poor. Relying entirely on her personal means and the care of God, Trotter founded the Algiers Mission Band, which survives today as the Arab World Ministries.

Her ministry as a compassionate figure to the poor was remarkable among the Algerians, yet it was her aura as a spiritual person that drew the most attention. In 1902 Trotter was invited to the *zaouria*, a fraternity house of the Sufi brotherhood, to discuss contemplative prayer with them. Her book *The Way of the Sevenfold Secret*, first published in Arabic, was written to explain the sevenfold "I am" statements of Jesus to her Sufi countrymen. It became a classic in Trotter's era, published in English, Persian and French as well as the Arabic original.

Trotter displays for us a life of deep spiritual activity that was dynamic and engaging in the world. She was not a spiritual recluse or a

---

1. Richard J. Foster and Emilie Griffin, *Spiritual Classics* (San Francisco: Harper, 2000), pp. 86-92

2. Artwork by Lilias Trotter, *Parables of the Cross*, London & Edinburgh: Marshall Brothers, Ltd., c. 1900.

Lillias Trotter

contemplative monastic. Rather, her consistent practice of spiritual disciplines led her, propelled her, into the world to physically demonstrate the effects of a redeemed and committed life.

The classic book on spiritual disciplines in our era is Richard Foster's *Celebration of Discipline*.[3] Foster describes the impetus for this Christian classic as his first ministry in a small church in Southern California. After just three months, he had given them everything he knew. He describes his situation this way. "My problem was that what I did say had no power to help people. I had no substance, no depth. The people were starving for a word from God, and I had nothing to give them. Nothing."

Reading: Peterson, chapters 7-9

I'll take a guess that you will find these final three chapters the most accessible and most enjoyable in Peterson's book. That's all right. I did too. The fact that these were the most enjoyable chapters raises a nagging question. Why did Peterson make us wade through the meaty angles of prayer and scripture before he let us into the more accessible angle of spiritual direction? I think there was a method to Peterson's madness. Perhaps one cannot practice the art of spiritual direction until one first becomes a practitioner of prayer and scripture reading. Why? Because at the end (last page, first sentence) Peterson proclaims when we are involved with spiritual direction, "It is God with whom we have to do." How else do we turn our attention towards God if not through prayer and scripture reading?

A Look at Spiritual Disciplines

Spiritual disciplines are nothing less than the practice of our relationship with God. Too often we hear the art and practice of spiritual disciplines shrunk into the moniker of "personal quiet time." While quiet times of reflection in God's presence are certainly one aspect of spiritual life, somehow they lack the riotous expression of relational involvement of a Job, the deeply personal wrestling of a Jeremiah or even the pouting, escapist quality of a Jonah. If spiritual disciplines are the practice of relationship, these disciplines should be defining characteristics of our lives of faith.

When I speak of spiritual disciplines I am referring to an intentional, planned practice of relation that leads to spiritual maturity in specific and measurable ways. These practices go beyond, "I want to spend ten minutes praying every day." Why do you want to pray? What impact will such prayer have on your life? What need for the world is God directing you towards that only he will fulfill as you practice prayer obedience to

---

3. Richard J. Foster, *Celebration of Discipline: The Path to Spiritual Growth*, (San Francisco: Harper, 1978).

him? Spiritual disciplines are not practices for our good alone. Spiritual disciplines are practiced for the good of the world.

Action Step

Turn to page 16 in your personal answer book and consider your spiritual disciplines. What spiritual disciplines do you regularly practice for spiritual health and vitality? The following two lists look at disciplines of engagement and disciplines that call for letting go. These are not comprehensive lists of spiritual disciplines, yet they are representative. Check only those for which you have a thoughtful plan and practice.

Disciplines of Engagement/Activity

Scripture Study/Meditation: Spending time reading scripture and meditating on its meaning and importance in my life in order to cleanse my body and mind.

Scripture Memorization: Memorizing the Bible in order to conform my heart and transform my thoughts.

Worship: Offering praise and adoration to God in order to give my life perspective.

Prayer: Talking and listening to God about my relationship with him and my needs in order to learn how to trust Him as source and provider.

Thankfulness: Spending time focusing on what God has done for me and thanking Him so that I become a person of thankful response.

Fellowship: Mutual caring and ministry in the body of Christ through committed, accountable relationships so that I live responsibly towards myself, my family and my Christian brothers and sisters.

Confession: Regularly confessing my sins to the Lord and other trusted individuals in order to experience God's forgiveness and cleansing.

Discernment: Giving attention to what God is doing or wanting in the person who is before me at any given moment.

Disciplines of Letting Go/Abstinence

- **Submission:** Humbling myself before God and others while seeking accountability in relationships.
- **Solitude:** Spending time alone with God as my focus.
- **Silence:** Removing noisy distractions so I become better able to hear God.
- **Slowing Down:** Putting myself in situations where I have to move at a slower pace to break the hurriedness in my life.
- **Fasting:** Skipping a meal(s) (or abstaining from an activity) so I

learn to find greater nourishment from God.

- **Secrecy:** Avoiding self-promotion, practicing serving God without others knowing so that service flows out of who I am as God's son or daughter.

- **Frugality/Sacrifice:** Choosing to live with less money and still meet my basic needs as a practice of my freedom to depend on God.

Action Step

Take what you would consider your top three spiritual disciplines, those that you practice most regularly following a definite plan. For each discipline describe the plan by which you practice that discipline and how that discipline leads you outside yourself to engage the world.

1. Discipline of

_____
_____
_____
_____
_____

2. Discipline of

_____
_____
_____
_____
_____

3. Discipline of

_____
_____
_____
_____
_____

Action Step

Over the next 6 months how do you want to improve your practice of spiritual disciplines? Write your plan below:

_____
_____
_____
_____
_____
_____
_____
_____
_____
_____

Prayer Team

Prayer is a spiritual discipline. What makes it a discipline is a plan to practice it. Go back to pages 22 and 23 of this workbook. Review your plan for your prayer team. How well is it working? What adjustments might you make in your plan in increase the benefits of this spiritual discipline?

_____
_____
_____
_____
_____
_____

Further reading on spiritual disciplines:

John Ortberg, *The Life You've Always Wanted: Spiritual Disciplines for Ordinary People*, Zondervan, 2002.

Dallas Willard, *The Spirit of the Disciplines: Understanding How God Changes Lives*, HarperOne, 1990.

Unit G
Strategy Assignment

The Strategy Assignment Overview

The Emerging Leader Training series is about development. It is designed to provide you the opportunity to focus on your life development as a godly leader. Each module culminates in a Strategy Assignment. The Strategy Assignment will engage you in a project or activity which will ask you to practice and reflect on one significant aspect of your leadership development.

Because the Strategy Assignment is more about development than accomplishment, please plan to give the appropriate time and attention to the process. You should be able to complete this assignment in three weeks. The following suggestions will help you gain the most from your Strategy Assignment:

- Read all the way through the Strategy Assignment one time to gain an overview before you begin active work on it.

- Plan a calendar. List the tasks you will do and assign dates by which you want to complete each task. You should plan to complete this strategy assignment in three weeks.

- Schedule a meeting with your missional director as you begin the assignment to talk over your strategy for completing it. Schedule a second meeting as you complete the strategy assignment to talk about what you have learned, what is working, and what is not working.

- Ask someone (your spouse, a close friend, a church leader) to be your traveling partner through the process. Plan times together with them to reflect and share. Open your heart to them so they can hear you talk through what is happening inside you. Let them hold you accountable. Let them support you, pray for you, and celebrate with you.

- When you finish your write-up on your Strategic Assignment, let your traveling partner read it for accuracy, completeness, and growth before you submit it. They may see and remember things you shared with them that you might have forgotten.

Personal Development Plan

Your Strategic Assignment for this Spiritual Foundations module is to write a Personal Development Plan (PDP) for your next season of growth as a godly leader.

In his book *The Making of a Leader*, Robert Clinton identifies two major lessons of leadership development:

1. Effective leaders recognize leadership selection and development as a priority function.

2. Effective leaders increasingly perceive their ministries in terms of a lifetime perspective.[1]

The PDP is an integrative tool that will help you begin and develop a lifelong learning strategy. Through the PDP you will see your life as a whole and prioritize strategies for working with God's intentions for your life so that you experience a satisfying life of being and doing. That is a lot to expect. Can it really happen? Yes, it can. The more you pay attention to the potentials and possibilities available to you the more you gain from God's divine relationship with you.

Here are some basic concepts to keep in mind when working on your PDP:[2]

- Lifelong learning is developmental in nature. It tends to follow the basic stages of life.

- Leaders are best served when they make decisions about life and ministry which flow from their understanding of what a sovereign God is doing in their lives.

- Our best learning and growing occurs when we are able to view our whole lives in one big picture that integrates the parts.

- Being responsible with our lives calls for a deep commitment to the developmental process for ourselves and those entrusted to our care as godly leaders, particularly our families and our church body.

- Finishing well in life is a somewhat rare occurrence. Leaders who do finish well tend to display consistent submission to spiritual authority along with discerning attention to their life flow.[3]

> YOU CAN EXPERIENCE A SATISFYING LIFE OF BEING AND DOING.

The PDP Worksheets

You will organize your PDP around seven areas of investigation. Each of these areas has a worksheet to help you gather and analyze the data from which you will design your PDP. Here are the worksheet topics:

---

1. J. Robert Clinton, *The Making of a Leader* (Colorado Springs: NavPress, 1988), 22.

2. The Antioch School of Church Planting and Leadership Development,, antiochschool.edu uses a life planning process called *Life N*. Robert J. Clinton's *Leadership Emergence Patterns* (Altadena, CA: Barnabas Resources, 1987), jrclintoninstitute.com, is another resource on life development processes

3. See Robert J. Clinton, *Finishing Well Factors: Enhancements and Barriers*, Barnabas Resources, jrclintoninstitute.com.

- **Clarify Purpose.** Identifying your purpose, discovering the potential towards which God is developing you.
- **Evaluate Experience.** Seeing your life story as a developmental process.
- **Identify Uniqueness.** Understanding your giftedness.
- **Define Identities.** Determining where you fit—framing your roles and responsibilities in relation to others around you.
- **Maximize Resources.** Envisioning your long term resources—your education, experience and work contributions.
- **Integrate Essentials.** Writing a Personal Life Mandate.
- **Acquire Wisdom.** Identifying what you need most from those whom God provides as mentors.

Writing your PDP

Your PDP will be a comprehensive (covers your stages of life) and integrated (reflects your roles and responsibilities) plan that contains your short term and long range goals and development activities. The goal is for you to have a usable tool you can refer to and modify again and again throughout your life.

You will develop your "first run" PDP in the final pages of your personal answer book. As you work through the following worksheets you will summarize your thinking in your answer book.

As you prepare to write your PDP into your personal answer book, keep these guiding principles in mind:

- **Be concise and clear.** Others, like your spouse and mentors should be able to understand your PDP in order to give you insight and response.
- **Be directive.** Your PDP should move you towards wise decisions, especially as you encounter unexpected life events that may change your directions and intentions. The purpose of the PDP is to help you develop as a leader through intentional insight and planning.
- **Be measurable.** Your PDP is a personal accountability tool. As you refer to your PDP each year, you should be able to measure your progress and see how much you have developed as God's person. Include annual reviews so you can know when you have met your goals, then update and expand your PDP.

You may find you wish to put your PDP into a different form or organize it in different ways. For instance, you may be very visual and want to use charts, graphs, tables, calendars, etc. on which to display your information. Or you may be a bullet point person. In that case an outline or bullets arranged under topic headings may be more useful. Other people might choose to write a narrative in order to capture details.

Whatever your style is, in the future you will have the main ingredients to develop your PDP into something that you use over a lifetime.

Remember to check your calendar and schedule a last meeting with your missional director.

My prayer is that your study of yourself in this Emerging Leader Training module on Spiritual Formation has been an enriching and eye-opening experience for you. I hope you know yourself much better now, and that you like what you see.

God is a God of the future. You are wonderfully made in his image, for his purposes. May God walk with you closely and may you hold onto him tightly as you live your life.

Worksheet 1 - Clarify Purpose: Surfacing Your Worldview Perspective

Use the following questions to surface insight about your personal identity and your purpose in your various communities. These statements will help to reveal the assumptions and values which summarize your worldview. A worldview focuses attention, integrates experiences, reinforces values and directs decisions. By helping you bring your implicit worldview thinking out to the surface you will be more capable of understanding your life development.

Expect to revisit this worksheet to review and refine it as you construct your PDP.

Who are you as a person? What is unique about you? What do you really believe about your personal identity?

_____
_____
_____
_____
_____
_____
_____
_____
_____

What have you learned from scripture, from your personal experience, from the experience of others about how God works in the world?

_____
_____
_____
_____
_____
_____
_____
_____

What have you learned about how you fit into God's purposes and activity in the world? How do your personality, life experiences, and giftedness intersect with God's will for the world?

_____
_____
_____
_____
_____
_____
_____
_____

What has become clear to you about the purposes and roles that God has for you? What are you capable of accomplishing in the world? What contributions can you see yourself making?

_____
_____
_____
_____
_____
_____
_____
_____

In light of your belief statements above, how would you summarize your worldview? What makes all the parts fit together for you?

_____
_____
_____
_____
_____
_____
_____

Turn to page 17 in your personal answer book and summarize your personal worldview.

Worksheet 2 - Evaluate Experience: Your Leadership Timeline

In the section *Your Walk With God*, you used Tony Stoltfuz's website to construct your personal calling journey timeline. Go back to your timeline and review it. It should be on page 8 of your personal answer book. In this worksheet you will look at your life more deeply to identify the major milestones, events, achievements and goals that make up the various eras of your life.

There are a number of ways a timeline could be organized (life stages, decades, education, etc.). The timeline you will use in this worksheet is based on Clinton's Ministry Timeline.[4] Clinton focuses on people in full time ministry, so he uses Ministry where I have inserted Leadership. I have made that switch to broaden our perspective on leadership, moving it from a church exclusive to a world inclusive perspective. I believe this world inclusive perspective displays more of a "kingdom of God" understanding. Whether your arena of leadership is primarily focused internal in the church or external to the world, you are an agent of God, influencing those around you towards God's intent for their lives. Clinton's general timeline is illustrated below:

Phase I	**Phase II**	**Phase III**	**Phase IV**
Leadership Foundations	Growing Leadership	Focused Leadership	Convergent Leadership

```
|_____|_____|_____|_____|
 A            B   A    B    C    A         B     A    B     C
     ---B1----         ----B2----      -----B3---
```

The timeline is divided into four development phases and each phase has sub-phases. Between phases there are boundaries, transition activities that must be accomplished before a leader moves into the next phase. These phases and sub-phases are explained below with approximate times in life in which they tend to occur. Remember, this is a generalized timeline. Each leader will experience these elements uniquely.

As you read these phases, use the worksheet on the following pages to take notes on your life. What events, experiences, and achievements have you experienced that come to mind? Think about people God has brought into your life. How have they influenced you? How have you influenced them? These people will give you a good clue as to what was going on in your life at that time.

---

4. J. Robert Clinton, *Strategic Concepts That Clarify a Focused Life* (Altadena, CA: Barnabas Resources, 1995, rev. 2005), 9.

Phase I: Leadership Foundations (first 20 years of life). Early shaping of one's character and personality as God providentially works through family, contextual background, and historical events. The potential leader's primary challenge is to respond positively to God's sovereign influence and take advantage of one's unique foundations.

A. Sovereign Foundations, the early shaping of our personality and character. Typically something we experience and share rather than plan.

B. Leadership Transition, a time when first leadership acts are made.

Phase I: Leadership Foundations (age up to 20). If you were to title this phase of your life, what title would you give it?

Leadership Foundations

_____
_____

A. Sovereign Foundations. Describe the major influences in your early life and how you see those laying a foundation for you. Some people have had very difficult early life experiences which make it harder for them to see God's sovereign activity. Remember, no matter what your early life experiences were, God will use them for good and for blessing.

_____
_____
_____
_____
_____
_____
_____
_____
_____
_____
_____
_____
_____

B. Leadership Transitions. This is when you began to perceive yourself as a leader. How did this happen? What roles were you fulfilling? What events occurred that demonstrated your abilities as a leader?

_____
_____
_____
_____
_____
_____
_____
_____
_____
_____
_____
_____
_____
_____
_____
_____

Phase II: Growing Leadership (approximately ages 20-30). Leadership initiatives occur as the leader looks toward the needs of others and causes that positively influence the world in godly directions. This phase involves experimenting with different contexts and developing personal giftedness. The developmental challenges are a) to recognize oneself as a leader for life and, b) to gain an experiential understanding of effective leadership in the kingdom of God.

B1. Logistic boundary, when initial leader assignments are accepted and the self-realization "I am a leader" is made.

   A. Provisional leadership, where leadership potential is discerned. Task is to form personal character.

   B. Growth leadership, where leadership assignments are taken on that grow and form giftedness. Giftedness and role issues are learned. Task is recognizing leadership potential.

   C. Competent leadership, when the leader operates out of giftedness in roles that fit that giftedness and produces excellent results. A philosophy of leadership is forming based on significant personal values.

Phase II: What title would you give this phase for your life?

_____

_____

B1: Logistic Boundary. What event, experience, or self-understanding occurred so that you realized you could and would lead others?

_____

_____

_____

_____

A. Provisional Leadership. What were some of your first leadership experiences? What did you learn from them, how did they shape your understanding of yourself as a leader and how did they form your character?

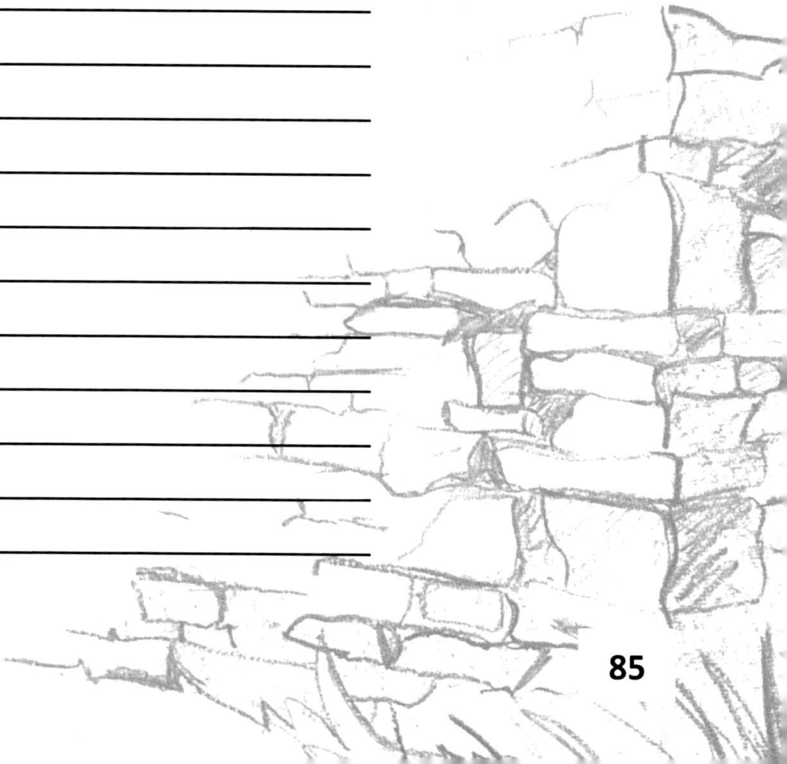

_____

_____

_____

_____

_____

_____

_____

_____

_____

_____

_____

_____

_____

B. Growth Leadership. What leadership assignments did you take on in these early years? How did you grow into these assignments? What gift items did you develop to be successful?

_____
_____
_____
_____
_____
_____
_____
_____
_____
_____
_____
_____
_____

C. Competent Leadership. What leadership role were you in when you first had the thrilling thought, "I can do this. I'm good at this!" How did this role influence you?

_____
_____
_____
_____
_____
_____
_____
_____
_____
_____
_____
_____
_____
_____
_____

You may have now covered the stages in your life. If you happen to be further along in your life development, the following descriptions will lead you into the next life stages.

Phase III: Focused Leadership (approximately ages 30-50). The leader is now aware of his or her giftedness set and is involved in leadership contexts and activities that are productive and satisfying. The developmental challenge is to deepen one's experiential understanding of God, resulting in mature fruitfulness, so that doing flows out of being.

B2. Strategic boundary. There is a deliberate acceptance and shaping of a role that is more ideally suited to giftedness and experience.

- A. Role transition, when there is shaping of the role so it is more ideally suited to the giftedness of the leader.
- B. Unique ministry, leadership effectiveness and efficiency is maximized as role, giftedness and experience converge. A sense of destiny, the conviction that God is preparing the leader for special purposes, may begin manifesting.

Phase IV: Convergent Leadership (ages 50-70). The time when life maturing and leadership maturing peak together in a role that frees the leader to use the best that leader has to offer. The leader is able to make a lasting contribution that distinguishes him or her through a personal legacy. The developmental challenge is to trust in God and to respond as God moves the leader toward maximized leadership. Clinton provides important insight into this phase saying, "Convergence is not something that one strives for but something that manifests itself as a leader keeps on being responsive to God."[5]

B3. Convergence boundary, a growing sense of destiny and ultimate contribution.

- A. Special guidance, movement is toward a role focusing on ultimate contribution.
- B. Convergent Leadership, as a sense of destiny solidifies that may become the driving force behind the leader's life.
- C. Consulting Leadership, when others recognize the unique contribution and capabilities in the leader they look to him or her for guidance and mentorship.[6]

As you reflect on your timeline, take care to make peace with the people and events in the past where you have been hurt, or even damaged. Bring your past constructively into your personal story. Use your timeline to determine your strengths and growth areas.

Turn to page 18 in your personal answer book and complete the information on your timeline.

---

5. Clinton, LEP, p. 49.
6. This is not part of Clinton's literature. It is informed by my experience in leadership.

Worksheet 3 - Identify Uniqueness: Understand Your Giftedness

Earlier you drew a picture of your giftedness set. In this worksheet you will pay attention to how your giftedness is displayed in the activities of your life.

If you find yourself more easily completing the worksheet on one side or the other, it may be due to some aspect of your personality or personal history. Make sure you give attention to your weaker side to get a complete picture of yourself. If you tend to be overly critical or overly generous with yourself regarding abilities and skills, use others' insights to help you be objective.

Work, hobbies, subjects or activities that you enjoy the **most**, naturally demonstrate the most skill in, and from which you get the most satisfaction.	Work, hobbies, subjects or activities that you enjoy the **least**, naturally demonstrate the least skill in, and from which you get the least satisfaction.
Work, hobbies, subjects or activities for which you get the **most** praise, compliments, or encouragement to continue on in that activity.	Work, hobbies, subjects or activities for which you get the **least** praise, compliments, or encouragement to continue on in that activity.

Answer these questions:

Look at the giftedness set you drew on page 15 of your personal answer book. With the new information from above are there any changes you would like to make in your giftedness set picture? Why? Go ahead and make those changes in your giftedness set picture on page 19 of your personal answer book.

_____
_____
_____
_____
_____
_____
_____
_____
_____
_____

How much do you seem to be working, acting and living from your giftedness?

_____
_____
_____
_____
_____
_____
_____
_____
_____
_____
_____
_____

Are you are gaining insight for the direction of your life? If you were asked to make a prediction for your life right now, like you might have done when graduating high school, what would that prediction be for ten years from now?

_____
_____
_____
_____
_____

You may be feeling a growing awareness of a sense of destiny to your life and some ultimate contributions that could be part of your life legacy. Based on what you know of yourself at this point in time, make a provisional statement about a sense of destiny and ultimate contributions.

_____
_____
_____
_____
_____
_____
_____
_____
_____
_____
_____
_____
_____
_____
_____
_____
_____
_____

Worksheet 4 - Define Identities: My Roles and Responsibilities

This worksheet will help you identify the basic categories of your life's social structure in terms of your roles and responsibilities. Use the following diagram as a guide for the basic categories of life. The diagram shows your life surrounded by your communities of family and faith. Around this tightly integrated center are your communities of friends, work and the world which are more differentiated from your core.

List all the roles you currently play within the categories of this structure. For example, in the My Life circle you may have roles such as: son/daughter, Christian, athlete, musician, innovator, entertainer, etc. In family you may be a father/mother, husband/wife, provider, homemaker, disciplinarian, etc. In your community faith example roles could be: minister, teacher, prayer warrior, mentor, etc. In your work community is where you will place your work roles. In your community of friends you might have roles such as humorist, collector (of people), organizer, play director, or any role that you fill among your friends. In the world around me roles could be missionary, builder, sustainer, philanthropist, etc.

What responsibilities do you have for each role as you see them within this framework?

My Life Roles

_____
_____
_____
_____

My Family Roles

_____
_____
_____
_____

My Community of Faith Roles

_____
_____
_____
_____

My Work Community Roles

_____
_____
_____
_____

My Community of Friends Roles

_____
_____
_____
_____

The World Around Me Roles

_____
_____
_____
_____

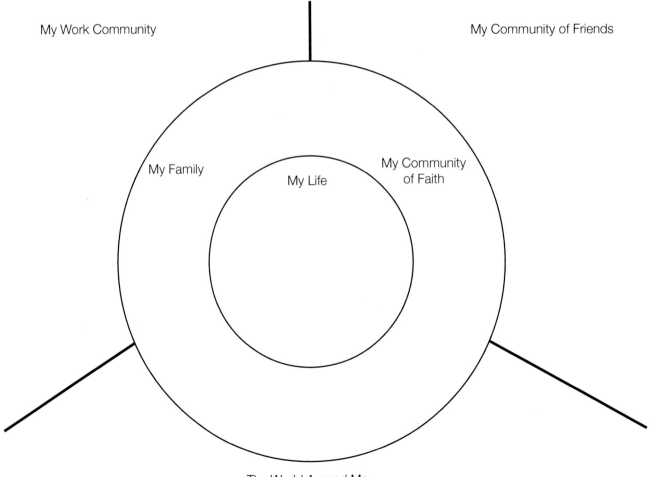

When you complete your life's social structure, answer the following questions:

Were you surprised by anything as you look at your completed role/responsibility profile?

_____
_____
_____
_____

What do you see about the balance and integration of your life's social structure? Are your roles and responsibilities balanced across all your communities?

_____
_____
_____
_____
_____
_____
_____
_____
_____
_____

If some areas are receiving more attention than others, consider the reasons for this. Is it because of a certain stage or time in your life? Are there special conditions that have required you to pay more attention to a certain area at this time?

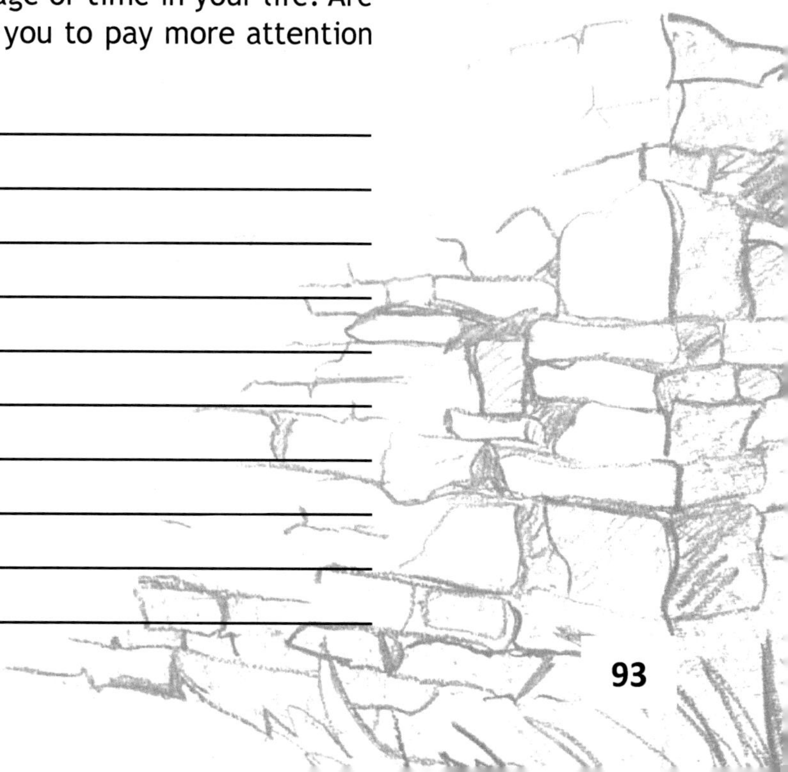

_____
_____
_____
_____
_____
_____
_____

If there are areas under-represented in your role/responsibility list, add some roles/responsibilities you would like to make as goals across the next year.

_____
_____
_____
_____
_____
_____
_____
_____

What observations would you like to make or lessons that you have learned from building your role/responsibility profile?

_____
_____
_____
_____
_____
_____
_____
_____
_____
_____
_____
_____
_____
_____
_____
_____

Turn to page 20 in your personal answer book. Look at your current roles. What goals would you like to pursue this year, the next 2-3 years, the next 5 years?

Worksheet 5 - Maximize Resources: Envision the Long Term

In this worksheet you will refine your timeline to focus more sharply on life resources. These resources include education, finances and life-work stewardship. You may want to break your timeline into the sub-phases to gain more perspective on your current and/or your next life stage.

Use the following categories and questions in your resource reflections:

Education. Place both your formal and non-formal experiences on the timeline.

a. What teachers or educational experiences were most influential on you? How did they influence you?

_____
_____
_____
_____
_____
_____
_____

b. What teachers or educational experiences were most difficult for you to learn from? Why do you think that was so?

_____
_____
_____
_____
_____
_____

c. Write the educational experiences you need to pursue to further your life goals. What will it require of you to successfully gain these experiences?

_____
_____
_____
_____

Finances. Identify on your timeline periods when your financial needs were adequately met and those times when they were not.

 a. What do you see about yourself when you compare your responses to times of plenty and times of scarcity?

_____
_____
_____
_____
_____

 b. How have your financial situations influenced your understanding of God's providing character?

_____
_____
_____
_____
_____

 d. What are your financial needs likely to be in the future and how do you plant to meet them?

_____
_____
_____
_____
_____

Lifework. Place your work experiences on the timeline with the length of employment identified by years (example:2009-2011).

 a. What were your most and least successful work experiences? Were they also your most and least satisfying work experiences? What made them so?

_____
_____
_____
_____
_____

b. Who served as models of lifework for you and what would you like modeled for you in the future? Who might serve as a future lifework model for you?

_____
_____
_____
_____
_____
_____

c. Identify what an ideal future lifework would be for you.

_____
_____
_____
_____
_____
_____
_____
_____
_____
_____
_____
_____
_____
_____
_____
_____
_____

In your personal answer book, pages 21-23, write down your goals for education, finances, and lifework.

Phase I	Phase II	Phase III	Phase IV
Leadership Foundations	Growing Leadership	Focused Leadership	Convergent Leadership

My next development stage is: _____

This is how I plan to work with God towards my next stage of development:

Education

_____
_____
_____

Finances

_____
_____
_____

Lifework

_____
_____
_____

Worksheet 6 - Integrate Essentials: Write a Personal Life Mandate

A Personal Life Mandate is a narrative which gives the essence of your life in terms of what God has shown you about your timeline, your giftedness, your major roles, and your goals. It gives you insight into how God will accomplish his goals.

Remember as you write your Personal Life Mandate that you are not just making a list of things you want to accomplish. A personal mandate is an attempt to bring God's preferred future into focus based on what he has already done in you.

Sample Personal Life Mandate, person age 30-40

At this point in time, based on what God has done in me thus far, I believe my life purpose will involve a cross-cultural ministry which will focus on high level influence, equipping leaders at both the individual and at organizational levels. This ministry will involve stepping out in faith and many times using modeling from my own life. I know, often, my ministry will be marked by unusual blessing of God.

I know that to carry out my ministry I will need to develop into an effective trainer who:

- has Spiritual Authority,
- can operate comfortably (design and/or participate) in a public ministry involving workshops, seminars, and conferences
- has an effective mentoring ministry (relational ministry) with individuals and in small groups.

I know also that I am to be a part of organizational influence, probably at a consulting level. I know that God frequently gives me strategic organizational input and I want to be able to speak this input into organizational situations to bring life and direction. It is unclear as yet but I may well start or stabilize several organizations over my lifetime.

Over the next several years I want to develop effectiveness as a trainer and pick up organizational skills. I already have small group skills and can influence small groups as well as train leaders for them. I already have found ways of designing and carrying out cross-cultural orientation and training for taking a group of emerging leaders into different cultures. I already have skills at leading and designing Bible studies for groups. In addition, I have learned how to design and teach several kinds of Bible studies. I have designed and taught integrated series.

My social base situation, single or married is uncertain at this time. In any case I want to prepare myself for ministry along the lines I have

> "WE DON'T KNOW WHAT WE NEED TO KNOW AND WE ARE NOT THE PEOPLE WE NEED TO BE. MAKES SETTING GOALS RATHER DIFFICULT."
>
> DR. MARK LAU BRANSON
> FEBRUARY 10 2012

described above so that in either case of social base I can effectively fulfill that for which I am and have been called to in ministry.

I have some indications already of ultimate contributions but I will not be focusing on these in the next 10 years as far as I can see.

Elements of your life mandate. What characterizes your lifelong ambitions and desires for lifelong accomplishment in terms of:

My life purpose:
_____
_____
_____
_____

Goals for the next period of my life:
_____
_____
_____
_____

Major roles I see myself filling:
_____
_____
_____
_____

Education and preparation I might need to accomplish this:
_____
_____
_____
_____

Family and financial situations that I want to see happen:
_____
_____
_____
_____

Write your provisional Personal Life Mandate in your personal answer book using page 24.

Worksheet 7 - Acquire Wisdom: Plan a Wisdom Future

In this worksheet you will identify people in the stages of your life who already have or who could serve as a coach or mentor.

Coaches and mentors are defined differently in different contexts. Here we define a coach as someone who helps you accomplish a task, project or other clearly identified purpose. Consider a coach as providing "focus wisdom."

A mentor helps you develop your personhood and character. Another way to look at the distinction between a coach and a mentor is that the coach's work is focused outward from your life while the mentor's work is focused inward into your life. Consider a mentor as providing general wisdom.

Both coaches and mentors are people on whom you will rely for information, insight and, most of all, wisdom. Sometimes you will be able to plan for specific wisdom input. At other times you will have to rely on opportunities as they emerge. The idea is to be intentional about seeking wisdom so that you are positioned to benefit from lifelong learning.

The table on the following page is organized by decades up through the sixties. For the decades you have already passed through or are in now list the roles and responsibilities for which you have received input from a coach or mentor and the person who provided you that wisdom. Use a **C** or a **M** to indicate whether that person was a coach or a mentor to you.

Using mentors and coaches will not guarantee growth or wisdom. But intentionally planning for opportunities and exposure to people of wisdom gives you the posture and attitude in which God's transforming movement can be manifest.

> REMEMBER... "SPIRITUAL LEADERSHIP EMERGES FROM OUR WILLINGNESS TO STAY INVOLVED WITH OUR OWN SOUL—THAT PLACE WHERE GOD'S SPIRIT IS AT WORK..."
>
> RUTH HALEY BARTON
> STRENGTHENING THE SOUL OF YOUR LEADERSHIP

Complete your Plan for a Wisdom Future on pages 26-27 of your personal answer book.

Decade	Purpose/Role Responsibility	Person/CM
teens		
twenties		
thirties		
forties		
fifties		
sixties		

Made in the USA
Las Vegas, NV
06 May 2022